"In Michael Salu's *Red Earth*, writing becomes a virtuosic act of listening. Salu listens to history's castoffs—slaves thrown overboard, soil used up and abandoned—so that the relationship between historical hierarchies of power and contemporary crises of ecology gently becomes obvious as if of its own accord. This amidst the strange and irresistible ether of Salu's polychronic forms and tones, as echoes of the *Divine Comedy* leak into the Orphic narrator's radio talk show. As in the classic novels of Daniela Hodrová and Ahmet Altan, Salu's floating polyrhythms seem almost to weave themselves, crossing historical eras, terrestrial deserts, ocean depths, and metaphysical thresholds—a polyphony of voices from all the dimensions of the world."
—MANDY-SUZANNE WONG, AUTHOR OF *THE BOX*

"*Red Earth* is a radio show on low frequency. Like a ghost walk at the crack of dawn it writes a different grounding and earth into being. Attuned to the quiet frequencies of colonial afterlives, our guides Manto and the narrator, descend into Hades like Orpheus, taking their listeners on a journey to hear the voices unheard in the earth—bony voices in the half light, raw with grief and petrified accounts of deep earth wounds. The methodological brief is to listen intently and hear in the earth different stories. In *Red Earth*, Michael Salu brings a warm and uncompromising look at pain, Christianity, the arts economy of 'black as bling', AI, virtual worldings, hardened realities and all the psychic contradictions of late-night colonial earth. Rather than the didactic pronouncements of terrible violence and its on-going presence, the writing bids us to come with, in an elegiac remonstration of the intimacies of encounters…*Red Earth* is a literary journey fellow with Aimé Césaire's *Notebook of a Return to my Native Land* and Franz Fanon's *Black Skins, White Masks*, and Salu's autoethnography is equally as impressive and unique in the tremor of its language and urgency of its questions. Stay tuned, a major talent has just launched a show that everyone should listen to."

—**KATHRYN YUSOFF, AUTHOR OF *A BILLION BLACK ANTHROPOCENES OR NONE***

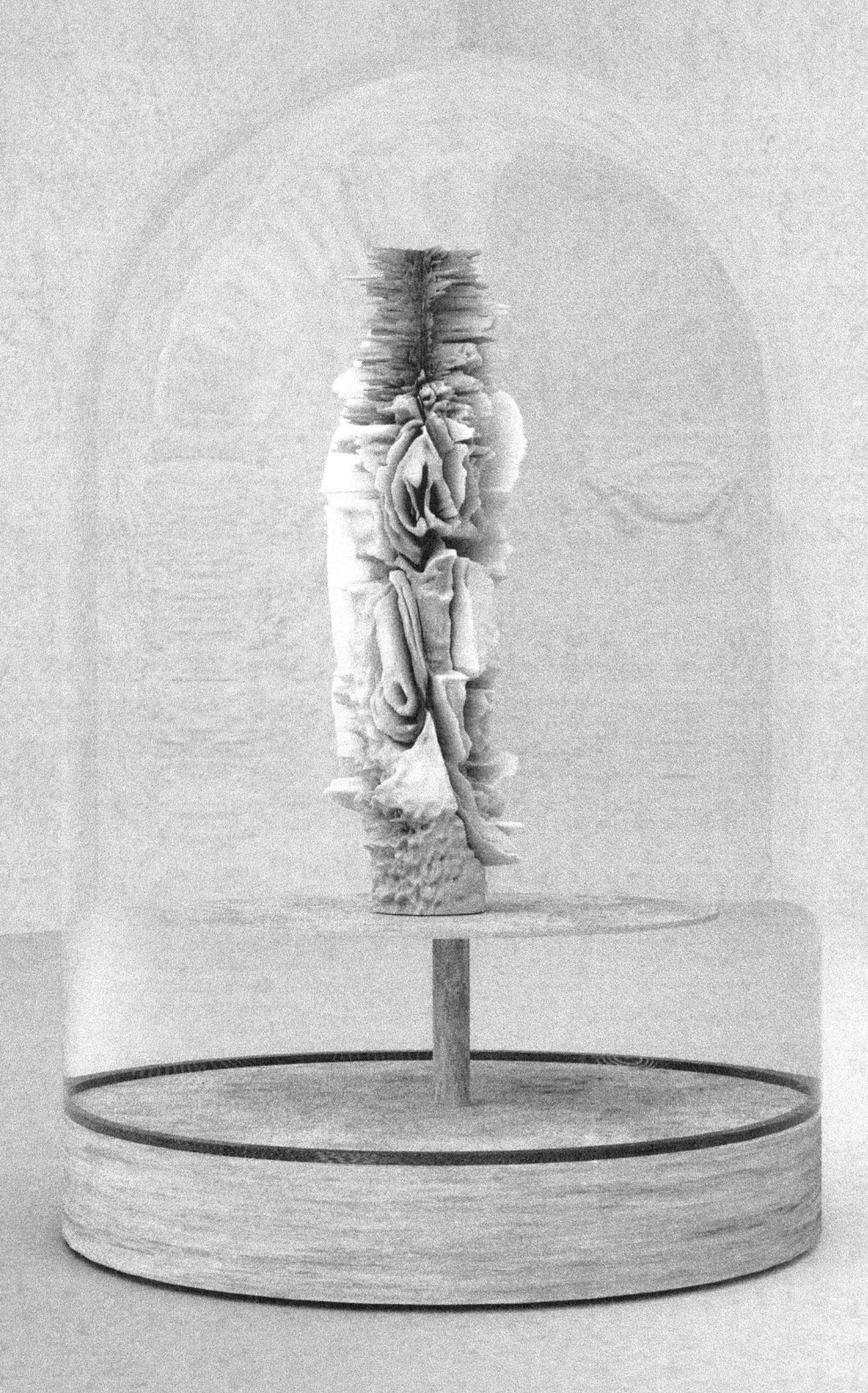

RED EARTH

MICHAEL SALU

RED EARTH

ISBN: 978 -1-940853-18-5

Cover and artworks by Michael Salu
theredearthproject.org

Cover

Ever Abeokuta

Mixed media: Photography. Text to image data translation from deep learning model. Virtually hand-modelled sculpture from data output. Digital collage. 53 x 83cm

Page 3

…Under the Care of… (detail)

Mixed media. Text to image data translation from deep learning model. Virtually hand-modelled sculpture from data output. Digital collage.

Page 8, 10, 83

Red Earth (detail)

Fine art print

41 x 26cm

Page 84, 85

Colonial Enterprise (detail)

Triptych. Fine art print. Mixed media: photography. Text to image data translation from deep learning model. Virtually hand-modelled sculpture from data output. Digital collage.

110cm x 40cm

Page 86, 122, 143, 144

Oya (detail)

Fine art print

41 x 26cm

Back Cover

Deference

Fine art print. Mixed media: Photography. Text to image data translation from deep learning model, to virtually hand-modelled sculpture from data output. Digital collage.

54cm x 74cm

PUBLISHED BY CALAMARI ARCHIVE, INK
NYC/BERLIN

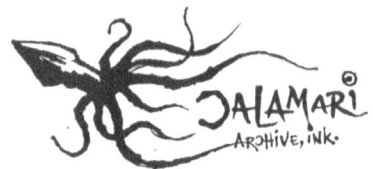

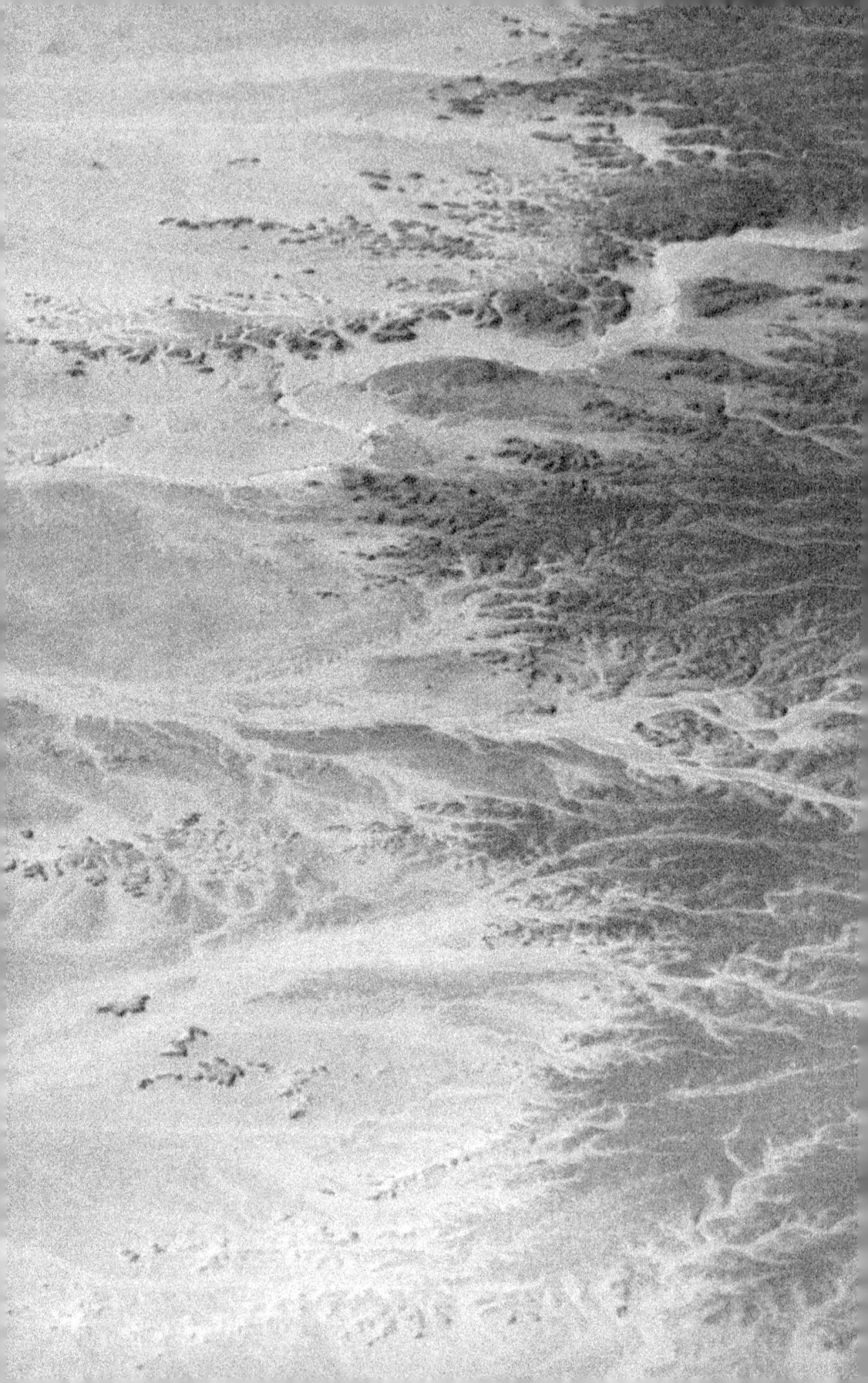

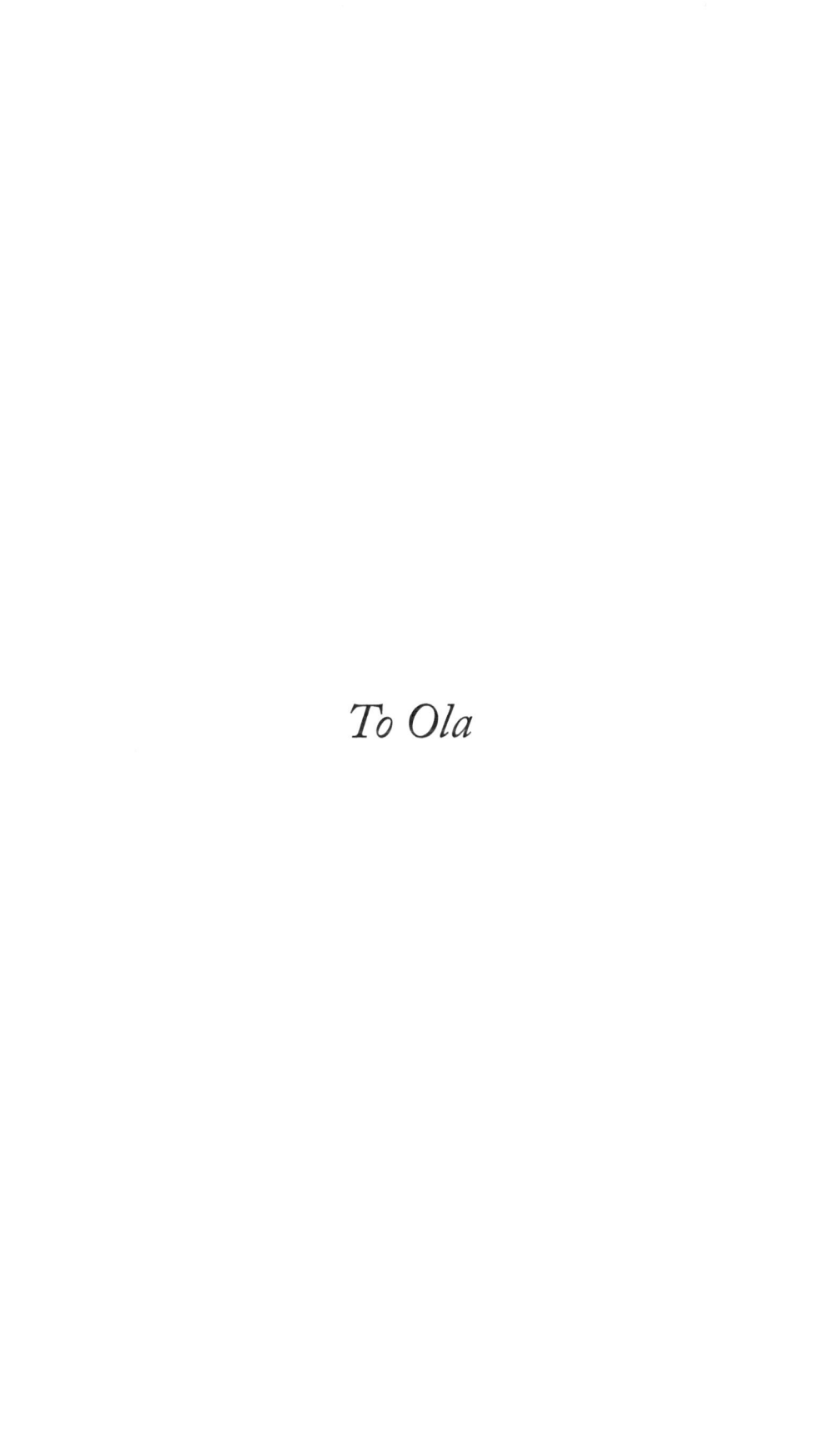

To Ola

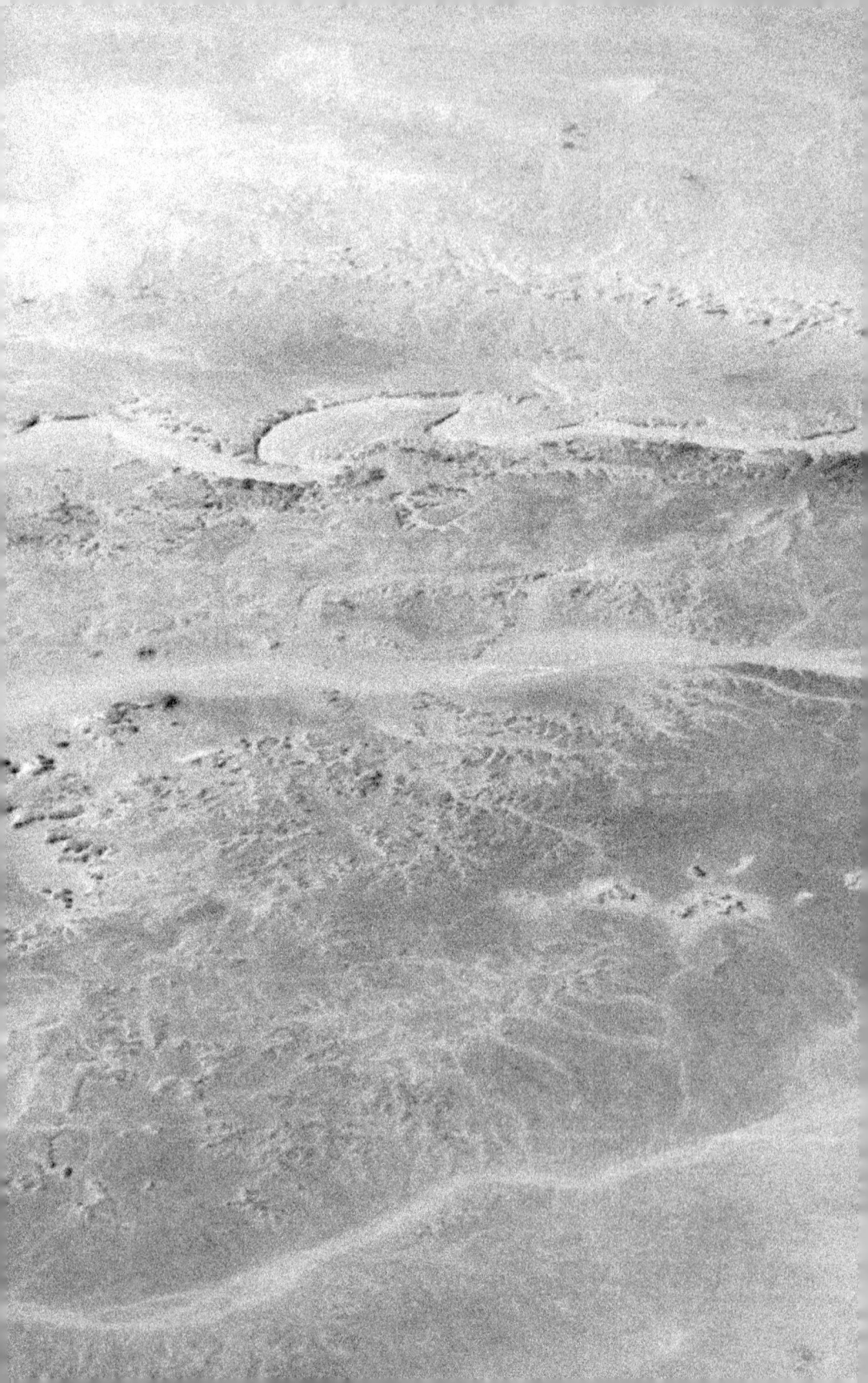

¶

Let us go home

where no pain can live

let us go home

where pain can only fall
from us to earth

Let us go home

When we remain home
pain won't find the curl of our blood

let us go home.

Let us go home

try to remember
where your home was buried

Someone said we live in words,
but yet with words we chase the indescribable,

not just in these words I offer, but within the torrid infinity
of words;

their combinations

their spaces

their geometric silences

their pauses.

Some may find voice in incomplete repetition of these objects. Black marks upon parchment, spittle caught by a bottom lip.

Muscles in our throats dance with air—undulations figuring out how and whom

We are given something, in a form we can add to, hone, and maybe pass on to a newborn.

'What is this?' I hear you cry. 'Another damn voice?' 'Enough!'. 'Who is it this time?'

Someone wishing good morning.

Or rather, 'Good Day'.

Better still, maybe just Good Being; wherever you may presently tune in, in whichever timezones we may now find each other.

Wherever sun sets for you, as how we once knew time melted. Where night and day made us offerings all at once.

Oh yes, Listener, be prepared! It is that kind of show! A radio wave formed of the lowest frequency, travelling through every dazzling formation of particles determining what drives us on.

Welcome! Welcome!

I am Ori, I am Head—your designated guide for this drive-time wander through the world beneath your memories.

While you sit nose to tail, mimetic endless strangers,

similarly entombed, each alone in immobility, we presume you might even welcome some company.

'Another show?' you cry again.
Yes, another show.

But, wait. Don't leave.

I will explain why you should stay.

You see, this here is *The Vestibule!* Which is unlike other shows, except in using a voice to tell a story, existing beyond the constant along with your ability to tune in to this voice. We hope you might stick around, possibly even participate in a talk show bold in our modes of travel.

Hmm, what's that you say, Manto?

Yes, I agree. Or even, rather, as my producer, Manto, suggests, we could be more bullish than this (as who else will sing our song?) and tell you *The Vestibule* is a show pulling no punches in our small attempt to witness unlit corners of our world ever-present within us, welcomely or not.

The Vestibule looks out with an open face—with reverence to our wondrous portion of the universe, experienced through the limitations of words, voices, and in this case, my voice.

With this the first of many shows (we hope), permit me a little oratorical indulgence.

If not me, then the voice granted to me, as it has travelled far to be here.

A voice which is—at least as I understand now in this frozen frame—an accumulation of moments and geological elements; like differing climates, or spirits mined from the earth and burnt into the sky, or shoals of fish drifting on currents passing through disintegrating coral, dispersed by danger and on to the abstraction of a coordinate—the abstraction of being somewhere.

A gust of wind upon a cheek. A dying wave creeping over one's toes, another death following closely behind.

A voice of altitudes and airborne flora, soon accompanied by layers of smoke from burning wood, metastasising into soil and its spirits, crumbling into smaller and smaller forms shaped by salt from the sea.

It always feels like accumulative vibrations hold in my voice's timbre—there, in each word, some I may have felt from a song sung through the dome of my mother's womb.

The song may be the cry of a jazz singer straining through some crackling speakers, a ghostly speck of textures past, hovering, while I made preparations within, the singer's words sprinkling an unborn with anguish and defiance potent enough to propel such a fiery desire to live in full. Such words could even have negotiated a path from a small television central to a living room, to nestle within my memories.

Words watching with interest while memories disassociated from the physical objects I would assign to them; like a photograph or a brooch or a toy car, into instead, compressed and uninhabited frames—ghoulish, programmatic husks of being. Rising like William Blake's *The Soul Hovering over the Body Reluctantly Parting with Life*—unwilling yet to leave. Instead, these memories lead me to a different way of existing, which I will not again consult, becoming something virtual and away from me, to nothing.

External memories lying dormant, no longer recalled, but in their inertia leave trace remains of words I can find to shape into something new.

Like words spoken beneath a Pawpaw tree, where my mother might have stood as a young girl, gossiping with her friends about what occurred during last night's party.

Where the sound system crackled and the bass it proffered gave the unlit earth a noticeable hum, and voices scattered out through the dark. The occasional flash of a lighter catching a bright smile.

Or they could be words gathered in a long string of names as gifted to a Yoruba child on their eighth day in this world, and found in the joyous chorus holding the child aloft.
Repeating.
Repeating.
Ringing in celebratory mouths and ears gathered with care around the mother and her newborn.

Well-wishers arrange spherically like fluffy dandelion seeds perching lightly on the head of their flower; their attention is drawn to the centre, where the child nestles snugly against the bosom. Each shields the baby, guiding the new world's gaze, delighted at this arrival.

This child will remain nameless until its eighth day of breathing this air, as the child is not yet of this new world and is waiting, in the vestibule, amidst their goodbyes to the previous world.

I imagine how those eight days can quickly slip through one's grip. The first might well up remote awareness of an end becoming a possibility, or at least a change, some kind of rupture, but on this first day, it is an end distant enough for the child and those they share moments with to dance in the joy of now.

So they will enjoy the sharp dry rosé from an elegant bottle with a long curved neck like a swan.

They'll bring a fresh salad to a garden table dressed

wantonly by leaves fallen from the olive tree, sheltering them a little from the season.

Another day might lead them on a light stroll away from their grounds, taking them deep into the surrounding forest, necks warming under dappled rays from a sun hotter and less inhibited than they have ever known it to be.

They could pause on their backs amongst long grasses central to a clearing of tall trees and tilt their heads up to look at what is above.

The unborn child might then be hit with a sudden yet simple revelation; that this new world they are to enter exists upside down.

Everything does. The trees, respiratory monuments fixed to the earth's spherical surface, oceans housing all manner of life we've yet to meet.

How we sprout out from this layered sphere of materials; architectural mimesis, possibly—tiny organisms ogled under a microscope.

Just like the earth's clusters of respiratory apparatus jutting outwards, the reaching tendrils of an organism float in the preservation fluid of the universe, orbiting its life force at speed.

The child would keep this sudden discovery to themself, thinking about how gravity can pin us down against this hurtling rock and transform how and what we perceive.

They would think about how gravity can hold a vast ocean in place as it does our illusory existence aboveground and where we fall and become a food source when our bodies crumble in death, which is a story that can only be a fallacy.

The child will discover that things, in fact, are the other way around to how we insisted this story is to be told, and in the cold truth of language, a browning, crisping, disintegrating corpse does, instead, float upwards—tiny fragments that rest on the top layer of earth, a layer of the dead, feeding the new life to come.

Will this corpse then join the cosmos itself? Will it watch its dispersal into all that is above, absorbing its tiny grains, its shedding skin as continuity of being?

Soon it would be time for the child to say goodbye. Silence will befall those they will leave behind.

Even a suitcase belonging to the child will express defiance. An errant trouser leg will aim at martyrdom as it obstructs closure, only to delay the inevitable, but this is not a sign.

Voices overlap, selfhood shifts. Caught in the multiplicity of a flock of birds lifting off together, their wings sometimes overlapping, whirling up powerful physics of a collective motion beyond aerodynamic drag.

Here some will lead, others will gratefully follow, clutching at simpler air provided as they head southward and away from sparsely populated grounds beginning to dampen and freeze, on down to warmer lands, passing over the Mediterranean, where, lying at the bottom of this sea among the furry rock, are stories; loves, griefs and grievances of the past in the bones of Phoenicians or Mesopotamians. Shards from the hulls of ships jut out from the seabed, pointing at all that is yet to occur.

Decanted from mercenary vessels, bodies of darker hues clamber and fret through turbulent waters to the shore. Gulps of seawater hasten exhaustion. They glimpse the bright
vacant
sandy beach
on the horizon. Their salted limbs gain weight, and their resolve diminishes into a million tiny pieces of rock. Millions of years of erosion.

Some drag themselves onto tiny grains of bodies past. Some float to dry land or onto countless crustacean remains that fought battles and self-amputated limbs for survival, as a defence against fallibility, to regrow and regroup.

Sorry, Listeners. Goodness, I drift, but I did say this is a show unlike other shows. Come, as we wander.

Please sit back, and allow my excellent producer, Manto, and I to take you on the journey only a low-frequency radio show can go.

What is that you say, Manto? OK, yes, noted. I will.

As you might have guessed, Listeners, my partner, Manto, does not speak, or rather they do, but they speak through me. We work together, thought and voice.

Manto would like me to inform you this is a show where

time reveals its foreverness and nothingness. Where time happens all at once.

The Vestibule, a show reminding us we had always thought of time as what came before and what will then come, and that, no, this is likely untrue.

Instead (and I offer this without assertion, so be kind), maybe time is where we sit dining at an endless feast abundant with flowing jugs of wine and fish fresh from South Atlantic seas.

A thinlip mullet fish caught from its once-clean waters. We flay its soft, placid white flesh atop a bed of fragrant polenta.

It is where we pass an array of aromatic dishes around the table amongst those of us no longer of flesh but who once lived to give us a voice and, in no hollow sense, helped us live.

So where do I begin, Listeners?

I could open, I suppose, by describing what I currently see before me.

It is early sunrise where I look out; the sky is alight with a thick band of red burning through the clouds, glittering their edges until they resemble hot metals.

All this while we sleep. Mostly we sleep.

Though some of us will not or cannot sleep, but lie there with eyes burnt open, wide awake, our bodies tossing and turning, sweat glistening our foreheads, dripping behind our temples and our conscience, onto soft down pillows beneath those of us fortunate enough to sleep like this.

Because, really, how can we sleep? The earth is too awake to sleep; instead, our late-night thinking thickens the air.

Our minds busy with codes left in our bodies.

Our bodies restless with scars carved into our minds.

We lie awake yet find we can travel the quiet, pockmarked, frugally lit streets—our fingertips lightly brush topsides of leaves as we float by, and trees whisper ever so quietly because there's no wind this time of year to carry forth their wisdom through the stultifying heat.

Come now as we float through night upside down—gravity located and named—on down to penal hallways when it is 'lights out', but many eyes of those at rest are also fixed open.

They don't sleep.

Our fingers graze the metal bars of their cages, a soft melodic thud, metallic, tap-tap-tap, scattered lightly over the skin of a drum.

Ears prick.

Who hears tap-tap-tap but the prisoner shivering alone in the bleak, wrapped in sweat that does not 'wick away'. Sweat of withdrawal from the world.

The prisoner shifts in a recess in the centre of his mattress, where wooden slats beneath him have long since rotted with damp; his spine sunken, night after night devoid of support, becoming a permanent lumbar concern.

The tap-tap-tap echoes assisted by hard cold walls—a hopeful polyphony.

The prisoner knows we are there, Listeners. He knows we have passed by and will come again.

We say, 'friend'. The prisoner drums lightly on the bed frame with his fingers, inaudible to most, yet we can feel it.

Boxed in, he drums, night after night on the brittle surface. He knows which divots trigger which vibrato; he plays, melody evolves over time, which now he understands as something beyond him, static yet infinite and will never move, not for him.

He fights.

He fights shedding tears.

He fights certainty.

He fights for his isolation to become some kind of sacrality.

Nightly, dead skin falls from his body. Life force is given to slow disintegration, his temporality reaping gain for another, like wheat sowed as his body atrophies. We fail to observe the slow death of a houseplant, imperceptible to the limits of one's sight, an unfathomable experience of time.

Like how a dog to us might appear to have had a short life, but to the dog, this life was full and overwhelmingly rich. Watch the dog for a moment, one that has chosen your company. Its unrelenting range of sensations is an experience of heightened, constant living that seems nearer to the intensity of our orgasm. Twenty years of this is surely enough.

Listeners, I tap my fingers lightly on this wooden surface. Tiny vibrations are emitted, some of which I feel in my body, but I'm unfortunately unable to see the clear line I believe should unfold through my past and ancient rhythm.

Are you still with me, Listener? I hope so.

Maybe you're now looking alongside me at rusting hulks of dead industries reclaimed by the spirit of our artists, those expanses of land peppered with industrial relics. Why do they treat their home as they do?

We observe how artists re-inhabit abandoned skeletal structures, building homes anew, filling them with life for a time. A swarming species finds a new nest.

So much has passed by these lands, perishing them of life, purpose drained away with the soil's virility.

Steeples that once coughed burnt earth into the atmosphere now sit dormant, smokeless, monuments to a way of living some of us are trying to leave behind.

People left as the work did.

Those who remained withered where they sat; their attention bought and borne as tithes to be redistributed amongst well-heeled lords and ladies of better-ordered classifications.

Slowly their bodies gave way, their ligaments waned, and their bones grew brittle. Their spinal cords stiffened, and their torsos hardened around old furniture—trees rooted to a spot long before unwieldy progress swept in.

How not to be cynical of those that consider themselves progressive? Those that will endeavour to refresh old lands first of all. Or those astute enough to notice the winds of change and rise early with the sun to position their masts accordingly, to catch the first gusts of change still imperceptible to others. This practice, an art in itself. You are there, leading the charge, your voice heavy. Others listened, then followed you to this new, untouched bit of land and named you their king. The kind of self-serve we frame with the word 'art' is a talent from which ego may power the move, an orb within catching all the rays of adulation, leading one to be more daring and risk-taking. We're seduced, and form around everything we say which is tainted by its true desire, but words, the very substance upon which these words were recorded for eternity, is imbued only with the disingenuousness of false meaning. Which side of history do you want to be on, my friends?

Now, Listeners, across my view is a mosaic of cracked window panels aside an industrial building which resembles a stack of broken televisions.

As viewed from our vantage point, sprawling parking lots of empty malls seem to resemble the white chalk counts scrawled on the walls of our prisoner's cell. Don't you think, Listener?

Demarcations of cells, groupings of cells, bodies caged safely within the automobile, high above crunchy asphalt, a vehicle easily earmarked for death.

Tipped through a bollard into a ditch at the side of the road, engine still whirring furiously, smoke rising.

To think one person can even imprison another. To put a demarcated restriction around their existence, implying their existence occurs only within their body. As if their existence could occur only in relation to yours.

What happens to them when they are forgotten? What do they wake up thinking about in the morning when your stomach first rumbles? Do they read the morning paper alongside you or absent-mindedly spill a drop of your freshly squeezed juice on your white cotton tablecloth?

As if one person could just do this to another. Imagine that, Listeners. As if we could take away what determines another's existence and do so with impunity, backed by a structured network of humans; gleaming, polished nodes gathered in clusters, gaining in power enough to strip away an individual's autonomy, their dignity, their humanity. Yes. This is why you do it, right?

It is of the same infrastructural legacy, fearfully maintaining the elevation of a certain kind of body and mind. Dehumanising practices are of our every day, and how we celebrate our ability to render them invisible, even in close proximity.

And yet, they are here, still unbroken.

Counting down days, weeks, months, and lives. Counting erasure.

Above us, the aforementioned sun hovers authoritatively, dismissive of the night's impudence, whose attempts to take over day always seem to fall short.

Bleary-eyed. An empty whiskey glass. A clogged left nostril.

Smoke clouds hang low in a living room. Conversations mute and unmute, possibly slipping to delirium or a fumble of limbs, attempts to devour the best of night's kindly disguise.

A mouse scampers gratefully between pairs of hobbling legs, and morsels of cheese fall loudly on the floor.

And how a variety of toppings slide off late-night pizzas stuffed into mouths agape at what night offered them and pupils dilate under the unforgiving fluorescent light of the pizzeria.

Someone chugs. Someone else laughs. A siren goes ignored.

Here in the night, they want to love you cravenly, and they want to drink you in, and stickily cover themselves with you. During the day, it would be different; then, they would only stare broodingly, with distrust.

The cover of darkness offers the truth of desire; fantasy takes a gilded mirror to daytime anxieties and scapegoating. Night brings down masks; plastic, leather, fabric, or latex. Chemicals swirl in mouths, switching real-world for dream-world.

Can you tell me, Listeners, what happens when the night is no longer available to us? Where will we hide?

Night comes with an accompanying soundtrack.

The light tap of a fox's paws on concrete. People flow from their homes, comforts sought under a dark sky, which remains forgiving.

We'll see neon burn from the ground floor of an apartment block. There goes a man, staggering. Parking himself on a bench. Fingers shaking a little, yet rolling a cigarette. Light paper crackles; see him pause, tobacco flitting in the breeze of this warm night, some taking leave of the delicate parchment on his open palm. He will stare into space for a long moment, as if home, as if his eyes drift to regret or maybe relief.

He will not approach us.

Earthward-cast eyes.

Lips dry, quivering, on his old face.

Palpable hunger.

It is still night where I take you now, Dear Listeners, and I see a sizeable tea-light candle nearing its end on the dining table before me.

A small flame flickers on its tiny island in a pool of hot colourless wax. Suddenly a moth, in true kamikaze fashion, dives into the hot molten pool, seeking its end, yet this moth seems overwhelmed by its commitment to demise. The hot wax pool welcomes the moth, and one of its wings becomes aflame. I watch the moth submerge in its fiery hell, its antennae still aloft, twitching regrettably. Its wing remains alight; the scene is totemic. I watch sacrosanct flames on its wing undimmed. Shortly after, Listeners, now a smaller moth dive-bombs into the fire-water to its immediate death. Or so it appears. Possibly not. I watch with interest as its body seems to float purposefully in the direction of the larger sacrificial moth, as though unable to contain its desire for immolation beyond just its descent into the fire-water, along with the pioneering moth's still burning corpus. The flame of the moth's wing still burns healthily, flickering only at my small breaths of wonder at this ode to an ending. Except it isn't the end, Listeners. I thought there was nothing left to burn, that the flame would soon eat away the delicate film of the moth's wing, and yet the wing remains tipped by flame, somehow preserved by the fire-water and undimmed, seemingly not ready to 'lights out' this little pool of hell.

Others leave the table and gather around this garden's recently lit open fire. Nearby, I hear a nest of swallows as the chicks speak demandingly of their need to eat and grow, and the two doting parents dart back and forth dutifully. They vanish into the night sky for minutes at a time and return to stuff grubs into the open mouths of their infants, feeding and strengthening their bodies and their will against a reality that will mostly suffer fools.

They go unnoticed.

Colour slowly fills the sky and surrounds the stars. We peer through the gaps in the tree that shelters us a little too close to the open fire, and no one seems concerned.

Then it is morning again, shame it is morning again, as morning here brings into view how train tracks have collected deep dark orange rust from every wind, rain, and discord fallen upon steel that once underpinned the virility of this land—steel that had once transported blood and was ore for these tracks, lubricated by blood— a self-fulfilling prophecy of some kind. Tracks, valuable, delivering news and goods from elsewhere,

lie now

rusted.

Look closely, see blood,

traces in the morning when the sun is aloft and bright.

They said this blood did not dry but what was wet escaped into the atmosphere, to become ghosts.

What ghosts?

The ghosts—they said—hadn't ever left, remaining here, hovering alongside us. This is what I've heard, and want to understand evidence to support such claims.

Which ghosts are we able to see, I ask?

Those living and walking among us? Legacy in flesh and blood.

Or those, say, carved into igneous-rock surfaces, as vain yet inevitable attempts to mark territory thousands of years in existence before and beyond petulant, temporal flesh attached to brittle bones through which life will pulse only for a short, violent time before the bones relinquish their small voice to this orbiting formation of molten rock? Surfaces of mathematical patterning decorate time measuredly, spreading layers of hot, hot flowing earth, branching and snaking before settling into a form akin to the branches of trees or the tops of shrubbery.

Let us cast our eyes downwards, Listener, cut through this sizeable igneous rock, through discord, granite, down to mantle, and it gets hotter still.

Welcome currents down here, swirling us like ball bearings.

Allow this.

On we surge eyes down to iron and nickel, the valuable centre, the inner core and where we disperse.

Each of us held in place by heat, just vibrating.

It is pretty hot down here, Manto. Shall we have a drink? Something cold?

Manto nods in agreement, Listeners.

Look up and see where we have emerged.

As the red band of fire begins to fade from the sky, I scan lands where the earth itself is red. As if a fire is offered for sacrifice, pushed up from the core.

Here, land has been scorched by fires. Though not from natural inferno living beneath, nor fiery refresh of lands seething only when necessary, but by the intervention of men, who slash and burn and strip the land of its nourishing quality. Stripping bodies down through their naked flesh to the hardy nutritious bone.

'Pause', we hear an ancestor croak, 'there are practices, ancient practices we could learn anew, with which we might feed earth to eventually feed ourselves'.

Harmony disrupted, which saw a more equilibrial

relationship between soil, swine, and who stood on two legs and looked distantly across the horizon to flatness and first thought, 'There is more'. What happens, Listener, when there is no more?

The red earth is often inhospitable, requiring great care to encourage nurturing energy. Kick your bare feet through this red earth; coat your toes.

I knew the goat whose milk would have filled my child's belly. We need not have named her, she knew her way around.

Falling into now barren soil is our blood.

Ancestral blood.

Like remains of our bodies, plants die, their leaves and stalks wilt and crumble from green to an arid brittle light-brown that says, you are too late, dear, I have gone.

Now rest assured, it won't always be my voice guiding this journey, Listeners, my vanity is not without reflection.

For the opening show, it felt, well...

...vital for us to establish a bond with you, and we hope, you too will bond with our voice (and with us), and build something longer-lasting than green of summer leaves, and instead, more like eternal bark twisting underneath. I hope you think so too, dear Listener.

So thank you for tuning in to our inaugural show on your drive home from work. I hope you're drifting along with us, beyond steering wheel and air-con, if you have air-con.

It is another sweltering evening here in 'the real-life'.
'What is the real-life?' I hear you ask, Listener? Who is to say?

I can say with confidence, one shouldn't overdefine real life.

Certainly not in this heat, where form is slippery, where beads of moisture add sheen to our rage, where desires remain unobtainable on the horizon, glitching in the haze.

Real life switched places with dream life. Didn't you notice when that happened, dear Listener? Sleep became waking, waking became some kind of what we might call virtuality, and virtuality became dream.

On this pivot, a force led the spectre to fill my sky like a heavy cloud, and for the first time, dreams lingered longer than a blink upon waking. So deep into one's journey in a short life, this was witnessing a world anew, or discovering a world as one whole you had known of, but only through rumours, never firsthand.

Last night, I dreamt my father had gotten into a fight with a famous artist. My father and I had, at different moments in our lives, known this artist, independently, in the real life.

Yes, an actual physical fistfight between two old men, lumbering, and it was as strange as it sounds now, recollected here.

Although, as I retell this, more of the dream unfolds before me and I remember that moment; you know, The Moment?

Most of us have likely been there once or twice in our lives, where we encounter energy which will disintegrate everything we have been prior, and everything we might well be, and all present at this moment bear witness to such implosion, enthralled at the collective realisation that the subject has passed the point of no return.

It is when time is bludgeoned into a pause, and the men caught in this freeze-frame find themselves unwittingly reduced to a kind of primal autonomy, with the knowledge that they're stepping beyond a critical threshold. Yet, they grasp at a loss of the control shaping their understanding of how they have been designed to exist, whom they must mimic, codes that must be observed, and the violence they have had to serve.

The point of no return can sometimes unleash a comical scene, where clumsy shoving begins, onlookers observe hands flailing (however learned the pugilists) until one hand finds a way through to an embarrassing violence upon the opponent's face.

That's where I am now in my recalling of this dream.

I am looking at a face rumpling; the moment, the blow and the following expression.

Obscuring red mist.
Which is also disbelief.

Spray of blood rising to the temples, shivering limbs, loss of balance, awkward fall.

The particular sequence of frames depicting when power, frozen and exerted by two warriors, is equal.

A reach for success,
binarius,
caged,

to the demise of one and the ascension of the other.

A gripped neck.

Fingers squeezing blood from a face pinned to the ground, in submission and fatigue, a failure, a bloody failure of maladjusted bone arrangements, ligaments, muscles, adrenal latitudes, blood, cells—ultimately submission to a defeat.

I would share who the artist in question was, but maybe this isn't even relevant. My father was his opponent, which was interesting to me, given his absence from my childhood.

I have heard, Listener, fatherlessness can unleash imagination, so who was fighting whom?

Oh.

Oh. What's that? Oh really?

Manto tells me we have a caller! A caller? What do you mean? How? A Caller?

OK, but who can that be? We've yet to give out a number. Well, it seems we do have a Caller, Listener. What's that you say, Manto?

We have, Blessing…
…from…Badagry, Nigeria, on the line.
Hello, Blessing. What brings you to call in today?
Hello, Ori, and to Listeners of The Vestibule. Well, I'm not exactly from Badagry.

I am from the last place I was seen in the damp depths of the wooden ship.

Where I last looked into eyes of imprisoned bodies—my brothers and sisters; where we had lain so close, we'd keep each other warm with our breath; where our legs and arms were bound together as we crashed up against dead trees when waves licked at the boat and where I fell viciously sick upon my brothers and sisters shackled to me, strangers also; where they said I didn't have the strength to finish their journey to alien lands—I could only strain their resources.

They had insurance, they said.

So I am from the point where my body sank below waves, assisted by the weight of thick metal chains. An anchor took me to the seabed, mooring me to depth. Where I watched breath leave me in glassy baubles rising encased by the salty ocean, floating away from the carbon in which I rested.

This is where the ocean thickens, and my meat slowly cures and then disintegrates. I am softened, picked at by dwellers of seabed as I become entombed in salt with my memories. I lie with others that came to this; a final way of rest.

This is where I am from.

But not where you are, Blessing?

No, not where I am.

Where are you now? What have you been doing?

I have

              beneath the ocean
I then found

                           which we
              given to them

Blessing? Blessing? Oh, sorry, dear Listeners, it seems

Blessing has been cut off.

Shit.

Oh, I hope she returns...wow.

I'm sorry, Listeners, um, I guess I need to take a breath. What was that?

Manto, is there no sign of Blessing? No? Oh, what a shame. Who was she?

Manto tells me they don't know. The red button just flashed up. Maybe she will return to tell us the rest.

I need a moment. I will take a drink.
Blessing?

Where was I? Sorry, Listeners....

Oh, yes. The father, or at least absence of a father.

How is the space fatherlessness leaves to be filled? The lack of authority and subsequent experiences lead one to disdain authority, I suppose, but often constructively, filled with contempt for those ceasing or fleeing from their given responsibility.

Absence. Yes, absence. A series of voids in a tessellated pattern.

I think about what it means to be present as we traverse these lands together.

Does such absence contribute to our perpetual motion?

Although unlike migratory birds, we do not return, distances marked in sands too great, our wounds too deep to feel soil of home.

Maybe home really does exist only in motion.

Such disdain and distrust of authority can be scaled up to look at how we lived, never really believing in what one is told, diligence that we must apply health and body as fuel to maintain, sustain, and progress a rapacious and imbalanced survival system, in which some bodies fear, while others must prostrate, invisibly, as they find themselves, or more likely unbeknownst to them, they lie closer to the ground, becoming another protective layer of this earth. The haves reach away from the ground to the lighter, thinner, cleaner air, peering at the insignificant, a living top layer of earth, like coals flickering with enduring warmth to keep the fires of satellites lit, hot glimmering metals dusted off dirt, blood, and sweat and flung skyward and away to realise their god.

Yet flight to realising a god is not necessarily vertical.

You know, folks, I marvel at the simplicity of the Christian faith. How its mythology exists almost entirely on what isn't there.

The tomb was empty.

Manto is laughing at me, but seriously, think about it. Would I believe in you more if you weren't here, Manto? If I had known you or known about the idea of you, and you disappeared, would I not believe in the idea of you more than if I had seen you fade, watched your body decompose within the linen it was wrapped in? And how many times would I have needed to have seen and logged your disappearance? How many instances of your absence would be necessary to make me believe in what I could not see? We may ask the same questions about our code.

Manto is just shrugging at me, Listeners. I thought you were the brains of this operation?

They laugh.

How might I return to personal absence and cradle my void, guess its weight, arms wide and aloft, where I can almost feel the curvature of earth draw a line across my chest from fingertip to fingertip? The myth of what was supposedly there, so as I wander earth, passing through its familiar patterns and formations, we are low-frequency. My absence; a void hewn from earth, collecting and concealing mineral deposits.

Like ghosts remaining, invading bodies freshly arrived. Who won the fight? I'm afraid I cannot remember that part, Listeners, but the story of absence makes me think about selfhood, how in worlds we're each born into, we are taught of selfhood's essential position in understanding how we exist, yet nature so often says differently, clustering and sharing as much as it devours. Where we are primarily shaped—even if just at inception—by a mother and a father.

I think about how fungi spread as a mass from individual,

often barely perceptible, microscopic spores; nodes in a network, dots yet to join, or to develop a collective understanding of how to thrive. Fungi nurtured by wet earth fill out, synthesising colour and earthly flesh, burgeoning temporary collective resilience and knowledge, for a moment, slowly, becoming infinite, while merging with the atmosphere, again, tiny, imperceptible, but never alone.

What's that, Manto? Oh. It seems we have another caller. Listeners, this is really so strange. Our inaugural show was meant only as an introduction, consisting of my opening monologue, which I find I am lost in, pleasantly, but well, Manto, we fully intend to welcome guests on the show, so why not now? Why not respond to the moment? Who do we have on the line?

My name is Raya.

Hello, Raya, where are you calling in from?

I am calling from under a Rainbow Eucalyptus Tree.

A Rainbow Eucalyptus Tree? Well, Raya, I can't say I know that tree.

Yes, I understand. Maybe because this tree is native to my home.

Where is your home, Raya?

The island of Sumatra, in Indonesia.

Ah, Listeners. The Wonder! The wonder of timelessness. Welcome, Raya.

Thank you.

So tell me more about this tree you are sitting under.

It is an extraordinary tree. It has a very smooth bark that peels away often, revealing an array of unusual colours underneath.

Pinks, greens, oranges, and purples radiate from its body. It is quite magical. The richness of its skins.

It sounds incredible and a great place to sit.

It is. I do not leave.

I wouldn't leave either.

I do not leave, because it is where I was buried. Though my body is no more, my voice remains, living under this rainbow tree listening and learning from what the tree has seen, passing on what I learn to others able to hear. Others that might come sit at the roots of this tree.

It is where you were buried, Raya?

Yes, when too much blood left my body and the child growing within was killed by the man, my master, the man who brought along his one true god and son, both of whom

lived only in pages of a book and promised everything to enrich
our lives.

The tall, broad-shouldered man
whose yellow hair
shimmered
in bare sunlight
of our dry season.

In the book he showed to us, the book
he said we needed to learn and understand.
He showed us his god, a god, he said,
with eyes also blue and hair also yellow.

Please, go on.

The man that promised
everything and whom I was
to work for. He and his
wife, who was also tall, her

yellow hair longer, her eyes
filled with even more blue ice.

I was to clean and look after their church.
I would serve their food in silence;
they would rarely raise their eyes
to me, as if I was there, but not.

I stay under this rainbow
tree because this is where
my blood entered the earth.
The tree drank.

When they killed my baby, given
through violence to me by blue
-eyed man, this is where I bled,
where I rested.

My father tried to help. Tried to protect
his daughter, but he was up against

too much might, a magician's
might, that can make the horrors
of yellow-haired man disappear,
just like that.

Raya. I...

It is OK, you do not need to speak. We're given voice by what is
beyond the horror, not the horror itself, but I want to understand
this, this horror.

I wanted to call, to tell you to tell all of our stories. So where
these voices live on can be heard or felt in tremors within the
body. Yes, felt by all, even if they try their hardest to not hear or
to feel. We are here. I must go now. I must go.

Raya?

It appears she has gone. From this call but not from where
I suppose she lives, under the Rainbow Eucalyptus Tree,

which sounds incredible. Manto, please remind me to look it up.

Manto tells me it is incredible, Listeners, as if the rainbow tree is not of any tribe of trees we might know, or the responsibilities they may possess. This tree's vivid colours are the type usually reserved for blossom, but here, no. Explosions lie beneath the skin. Fascinating.

Manto tells me this technicolour does indeed lie beneath the bark, as Raya told us. Shards of colour pierce one's sight as if one were looking directly into the sun.

The tree sheds its gnarled bark in fragments, casting off the old, dispossessing what fades, husks out, and falls to nourish the ground below. How different parts of the rainbow tree's body age under the sun at differing speeds and uses of time. All the parts carry the legacies of exposure to heat, such an extraordinary discovery.

Seeing light as colours forming light, like a million tessellating pixels creating a rendition of itself—learning, speaking, thinking, and acting independently.

Like memories kept in our bodies, vessels transporting stories that don't seem to belong to us; instead, we hold them for a while.

The light is getting low up here, Listeners. I light us a candle. There are others remaining alight, remaining Blessing and Raya.

Manto has steered us to another touchpoint, and now, we float through seasons as we do the many times of the day, changing, retracing coordinates of shifting plates, glaciers creaking into freezing oceans, offering a haunted howl heard from way up here.

Where we can witness splintering ice and follow a departing floe, leaving where it was centred, wearing slowly into the blue waters diverging into smaller and smaller rivulets, moving between epoch-straddling formations of volcanic rock.

From below, heat rushes upwards to absorb the agency of this increasingly smaller ice floe.

Like upon where I stub my toe in winter, forgetting steel tracks beneath frozen snow when I walk across this abandoned land.

Manto says that must have hurt. Yes, it hurt, but I was numb to pain; the blood on those tracks, also frozen.

A particular part of what could be almost any city in the worlds we're most familiar.

A man is hidden in shadow from our 1:1 realities. He pushes along his home, a small home on wheels, full of belongings appearing as detritus to the untrained eye.

The man says the cart is populated with items keeping him alive.

In the cart is a small gas stove, a single pan, rusting, an empty gilded picture frame, a sodden blanket, a single shoe—discarded and then found—and an old 35mm camera. The man occasionally looks through its grubby viewfinder at a world smudged with grease and dirt from the speed of its living.

Sometimes, at rest, the man frames lives hurrying by through his viewfinder. He will patiently watch long takes of scurrying legs, darting here and there; minds uploaded elsewhere, separated from their bodies. He's blessed with a personal cinema right there on the street. Long Italian Neorealist takes. Long hair rippling in breeze, clipped by the viewfinder straight edges, with which he watches those that would not see him. A fashion shoot occurring, on the sidewalk, feet away, he sits, bigger cameras flash and burn. The model, dressed in swirling yellow dress, catches winds moulded to geometric shapes by structures towering up into the clouds. She stares directly into the camera, which in turn centres her in the world with flashes of light offering a halo, discarding slippage of her spirit in rapidly shifting poses. The man sitting on the street nearby looks through his own viewfinder and watches the movie constructed by an auteur keen on the awkward in-betweens, when and how society doesn't want to be seen, parts of existence we edit out. The man sees all of this; the model's rapid shift between poses, twists and turns, the momentary fail of a smile from her blushed lips, as her thoughts hover, elsewhere; the photographer finds his stance, tripping over the leg of the man sitting on the street that he will never see. Snaps happen in rapid succession, and then they are gone. The swirl of the yellow dress contained and wrapped in a puffy coat, swaddled against the harshening autumn winds. Man chews on the gum he had forgotten nestling in the corner of his mouth.

Underneath all the man's belongings in the cart lie three

tattered paperbacks he has kept for some time, discovered discarded in front of an apartment block.

No message left by those disposing of the literature. The books lay on a ground-floor windowsill exposed to elements accelerating their demise, eroding meaning, changing meaning.

Brittle ice settled upon books, rapidly spreading dramatic fractal formations across every surface, curling and crisping pages as fire also might do.

The man hoped these books hadn't gone unread, as he stared at the intriguing triptych of Ginsberg's *Howl*, Genet's *Our Lady of the Flowers*, and *Thunder Boy Jr.*, a children's book by Sherman Alexie.

The man flips to the back of *Thunder Boy*, imagining a well-read and 'well-bred' couple showering their only child with generosity of imagination and open intellect, bearing offerings from other worlds to wet his young mind.

He imagines they could have delighted in reading *Thunder Boy* to their child, a small story told from their ancestry and, momentarily, a way of being and belonging to the earth, which hadn't been wholly lost.

The man slipped all three books into his mobile home, where, now, they lived together.

Between the three, he'd read in a never ending loop, an odd page from Ginsberg, a chapter from Genet, sometimes even just peering at a single *Thunder Boy* illustration.

His imaginings onset a daze, transporting him to his mother's arms and words tumbling over him, as he gazed at the drawings, which came to life opened in wonderment enough for him to explore living amongst the loosely rendered plants and creatures.

I see the man now, Listeners. He trundles along. The wheels of his trolley-home creak and stick in the gravel. Tonight he searches for a dark corner to rest away from nocturnal eyes unable to see him, anyway, even when the sun is up.

Behind a diner, he passes two small merging clouds of cigarette smoke emitted from silhouettes paying him no mind as they brace themselves against the cold of a short break.

Now I...
It's another Caller, Listeners.

Manto says our caller does not give a name.
Sure, well, put through whoever they are.
This, now, quite the show.
Well, hello, Caller.

Hello.

What brings you to call in to *The Vestibule*?

I've been listening along.

You have? Excellent! I hope it has been a pleasant accompaniment to your day or night?

It has. I have a small, somewhat ancient radio in my trolley, and it only seems to offer a single frequency, and until now, it only seemed to pick up static and strange, well, like...textures.

As if the frequency was passing through matter like it had been tracing patterns and forms within our geology. Nevertheless, daily, I switch it on. Maybe I had hoped to hear something else, or perhaps I was soothed by those textures. I'm not sure, but your voice has accompanied my journey today.

I am glad you have found us. Your trolley, you say?

Yes, I believe I am the man you talk about, at least I was. You described the items I have in my trolley, though you neglected to mention the radio.

You appear to be describing the dark corners in which I wander, for the most part, unseen. This is my world now, a voice, only— no longer a body—living on in shadow.

I had frozen to death about a year ago if we're using old methods of time to validate a moment.

Or, like you say, maybe all this is happening at once, and there can only be now.

There can only be now. We can use a traditional comprehension of time if you prefer. Welcome...um...how should I refer to you?

Where I come from, my name evolves as I do. As a tree might or as igneous rock does over millennia. How is it you can see so much of me?

Well, friend, this is *The Vestibule*, a radio show that itself is a low-frequency wave, enabling us to travel through all the matter of which we are composed. It allows us to discover and rediscover stories. Stories are homes, and many have chosen to bury these homes of ours.

During this series of shows, we're setting out to take our Listeners on a meander through the underworld of a consciousness (or, should I say, unconsciousness) which is often denied.

I see. I guess this makes some strange kind of sense now, but equally, I must ask, what does this have to do with me?

I, er,
I.
I saw you,
I wanted to tell our Listeners about you.

There's nothing to know about me.

There isn't?
But...I...
but as we travel along,
I can see that there is.

You say this with such confidence. How do you know?

I...

I have listened, and appreciated your reflections, but I'm sure you know there is so much more.

More?

Yes. Did you tell your Listeners about the ones inside?

Inside...Caller?

Yes, inside. Inside the Listeners themselves. Underneath. Energy living within your Listeners, a disturbance.

An edge. Nervous energy.

You know what I mean. When something suddenly arrives to you peripherally. When an element of your immediate comfort is interrupted, a rupture created within what you consider natural order, slight motions you make between the vestibules of your linked tombs of home, car, work, home.

When something interrupts your mortal loop, you flinch. You are disturbed, taking flight, but unfortunately, this only occurs within. There is no escape.

Why do you flinch so?

What horrors give rise to your nervous energy and make you fear the dark?

What disconnects you from the echo of your footsteps? Like excess stimulants? Except this does not leave—a permanent heightened sense of dread.

The possibility that dread might emerge from shadows and take what it is owed, where it may reappear and give form to who and what was buried.

The petrified voices rise up from earth upon which your Listeners built their homes.

You should tell them these voices never perish, no matter how splattered their blood or scattered their bones.

These voices live on through whispers creeping between leaves of trees or in the defiant snort of a bison.

I believe your Listeners know what I am talking about, I believe they can hear these voices too.

They can?
Yes, they can.
I must go.

And here, Listeners, I find myself lost.

I thank our Caller, if he is still listening.

Now a moment springs to mind as if summoned.
I remember attending the first ever live show of a friend's band. A motley crew of excitable friends had gathered, clutching pints of watery beers, as we anticipated seeing

the band as something other than the friends we had known and as who they might become in performance.

We stood outside, some lit cigarettes, conversations floated above us, into the smoke.

My eye caught the eye of a young man. A boy, standing guard at the door, he'd been watching our little group with interest.

He was tall, well-built, and dark-skinned, in that rich way—birthed by the red earth. In that way, those that want to wilfully ignore his visible youth and naivety because they wrote him out of their language, the system they use to understand the world, and instead consider him older and possibly malevolent.

Hence, I thought, his likely somewhat blasé appointment by the proprietors as the face of fear to guard this establishment.

As cigarette butts were stubbed underfoot and the hubbub of voices filed into the establishment, the young man stopped me to talk for a moment. His eyes were bright, curious. He asked me what I did, who I was, who my friends were. I asked him why he was interested.

He told me he was looking for solutions, looking for a way forward, and we all looked like we were already somewhere. We all looked like we were from somewhere else (even though we lived in the same neighbourhood).

I told him what I did and what some of my friends did.

He told me he had completed a degree in journalism, but there didn't appear anywhere for him to turn. He told me about a feeling of futility keeping him and his dark face standing guard outside this venue, his dreams locked away, his hands numb and his body exposed to the winds coursing the earth.

I thought about what was clouding the agency he might find to navigate the steep path to somewhere else, to shelter. I thought about what stopped him from knowing where that path lay. I thought about who stood in front guarding that path, blocking his way.

And I realised later, much later, the young man had been trying to fill an absence and, if only momentarily, to find some hint of a forebear.

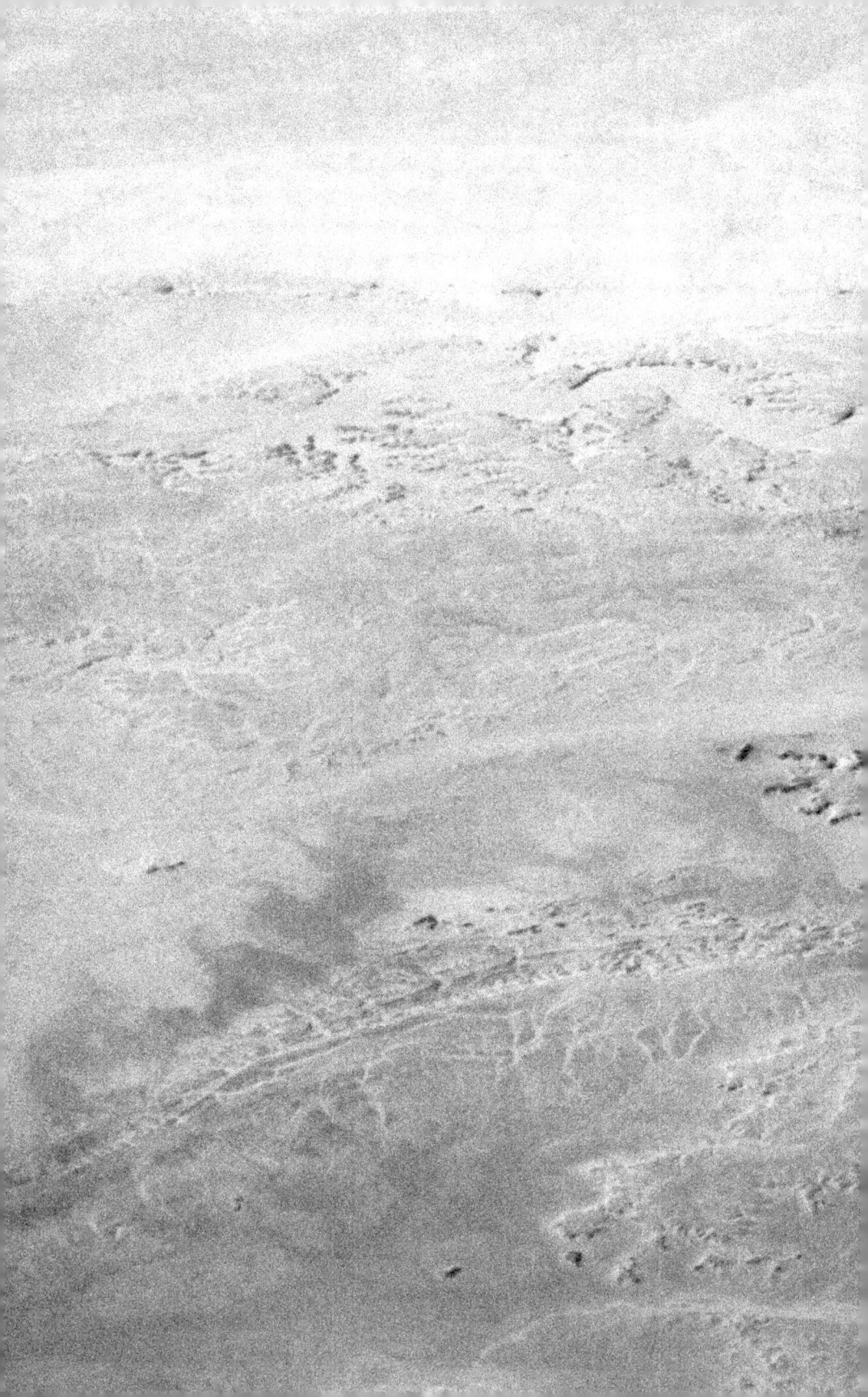

COME UNTO ME,

YOU REST

MATTHEW 11 : 28

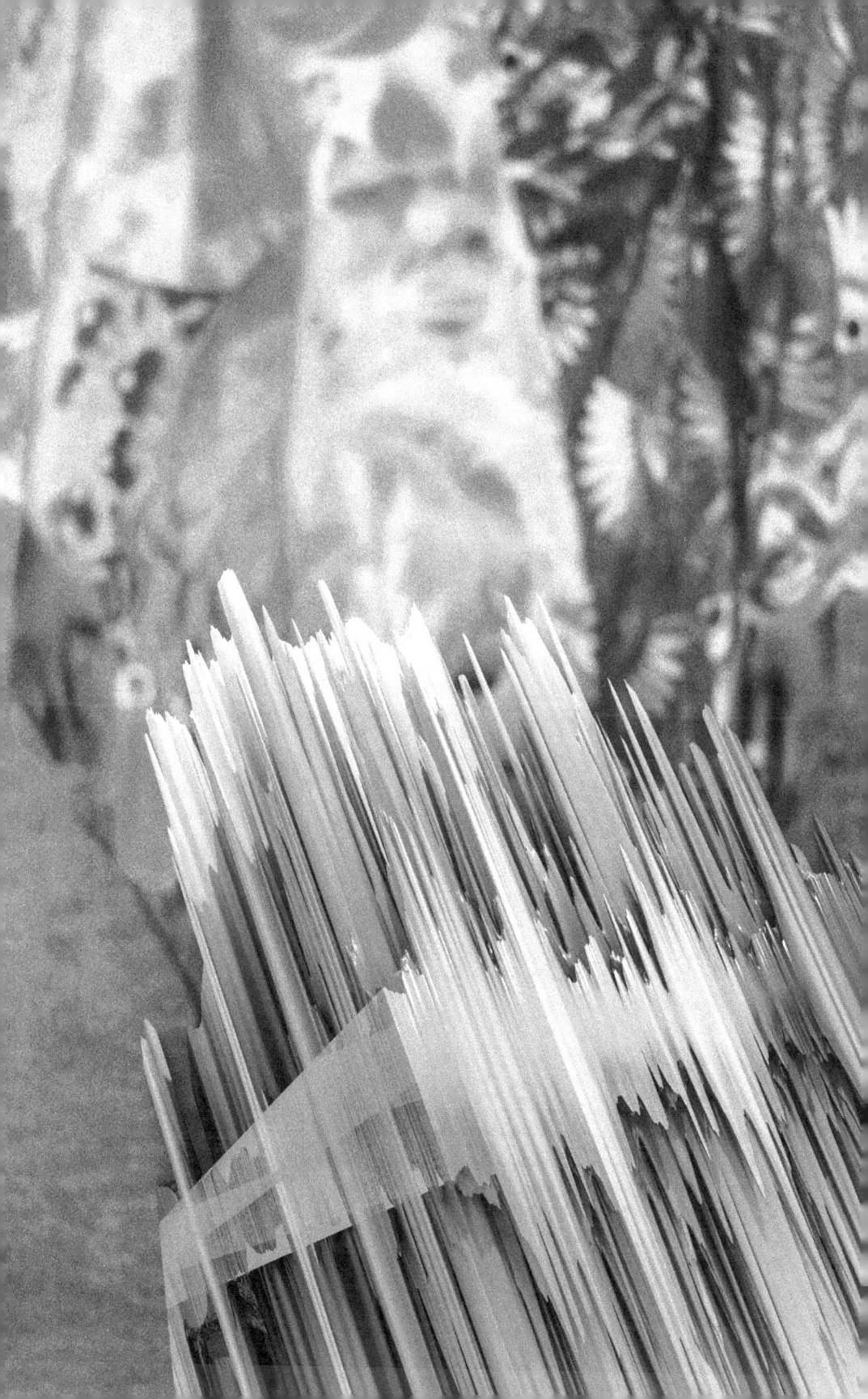

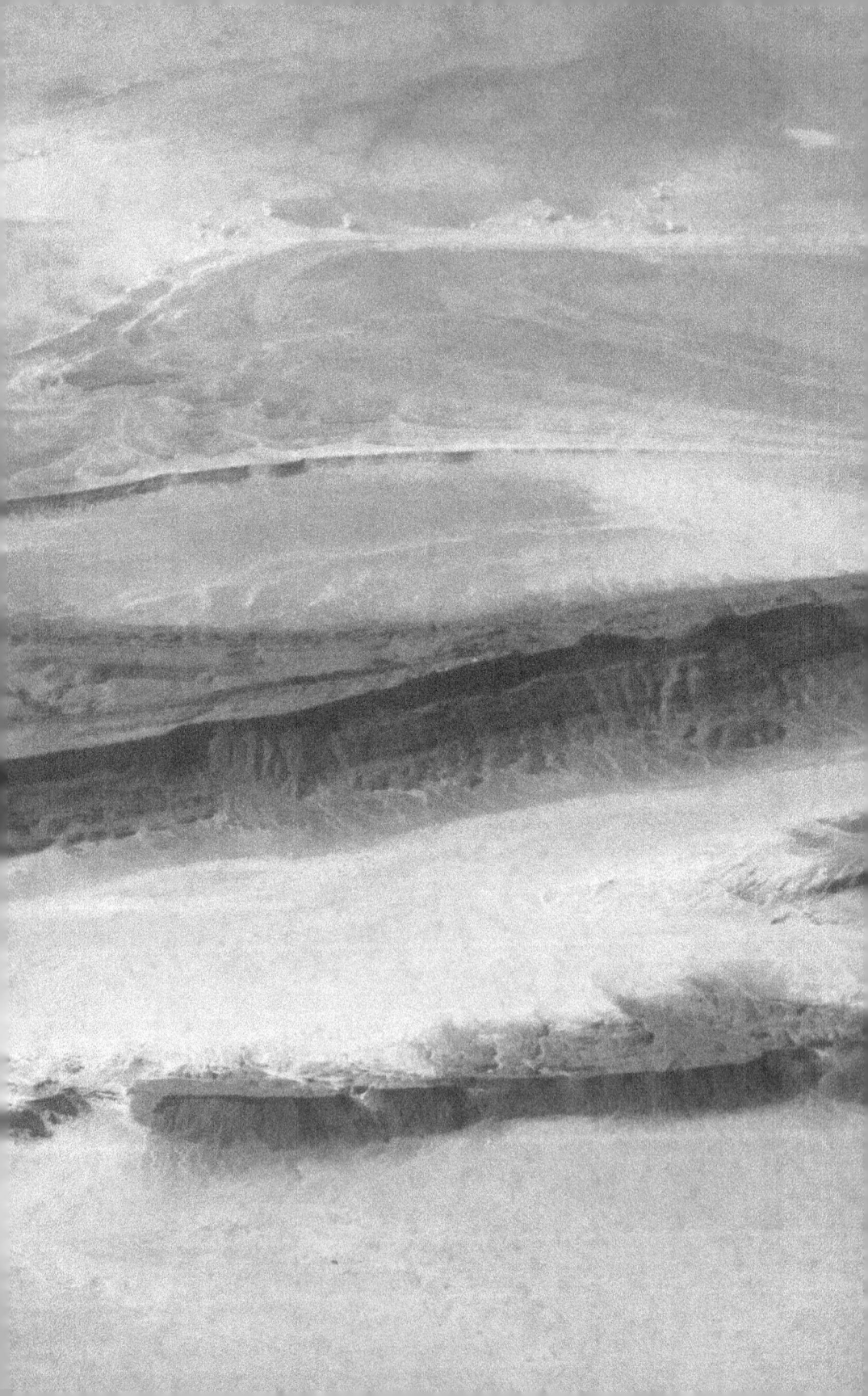

¶II

Thank you, Manto. What an opening show!

Yes, quite.

What will you do now?

How do you mean?

I mean now that we have completed our first show. What will you do?

I see. Nothing. Rest, maybe.

Yes, rest.

But first I will walk.

I will walk too, may I join you?

Of course, please.

Which way?

Over there and through the garden.

I like the garden.

Towards the back, where the garden begins to ignore the rules.

Do you see that row of bushes gradually overcoming order, where the pathway banks?

Yes.

I want to walk that way in a straight line and see what is beyond.

Sure, let's go.
So, tell me, what the hell was that?

I have no words.

Except it was not hell.

More like ashes scattered over soon to be fertile ground.

Yes. Quite like.
This wasn't anything to do with you?

No, what? No. How? I am as overwhelmed and confused as you likely are. I don't yet know what I heard and then saw as I travelled along with each of those voices and where they chose to take us. I am still thinking it through, aren't you? Didn't you feel they took us somewhere we always thought we could not go?

Yes, I do. Yet, they felt like places we knew and in some way had been to. I went to the bottom of the ocean with Blessing.

Yes, I did too. I felt myself float as if without a body. As if something loosened, a knot untied, my tongue got lighter, and my mind's sight filled only with nature. Watch your step.

Oh, thank you.

Like you said, about the way we floated by and the prisoner could feel us, our light call, tap-tap-tap.

Yes, but these were, of course, mostly your words.

I think now we share that space, don't you? We give what we have to offer all at once.

I very much enjoy and appreciate our collaboration.

As do I.

When those voices called, I thought about how it must be to live without bars, without a cage. How then does one interpret the world without limitation? I thought of bars as a kind of language. With words, one can carve deep grooves into the soul, wound and then harden with a recovering skin, but remain there indelibly. What can be a prison without bars? A prison building into your thoughts, preventing you from living or loving, stopping you from expressing true desires, preventing you from dreaming. How could the prisoner make love without pain? How will the prisoner make love without thinking of the numbers scarring their skin? What kind of love will the prisoner make? Can it only be a tragic love? Just a momentary balm, a touch therapeutic, but never actually a love with joy? When the prisoner is touched, will they wonder why or how they are touched? Could they consider themselves desired beings without the horror or negation of themselves built into language given to them, living in their bodies?

When I look into the mirror, do I see you or me?

It is a powerful constitution.

Then we have opened something. A door to somewhere. At the moment, my body retains nothing. It is tired, but a good tired. As though our Callers and our Listeners dissolved a cloud I stood within, a cloud which laboured my thoughts, and now, well, I haven't yet figured out how to behave.

They came, and they went. And yet a kind of presence remains, a phantom, a worn scar difficult to now point out on city streets of a darkened night without soul, amongst empty and hollowed-out buildings of history accompanying us as we walk… lingering.

I found it heartening they reached us. I hope they stay.

Yes, they will stay.

I say what you think, Manto, but nonetheless, it was reassuring to experience them in voice.

And it wasn't a dream.

And it wasn't a dream.

I was interested in where you were going with the dream about your father.

I am overwhelmed by my dreams at the moment.

How so?

At this moment, this midpoint in this body is the first time I have recalled my dreams upon waking.

The first time?

Yes, the first time. You can imagine, a whole other world has opened.

Yes, maybe it is?

Is what?

A whole other world.

Yes, how I also saw it. And the physical existence, which surrounds the body, appears to have shifted. It fell away.

Or to at least another cosmology. "The dream world switching places with the real world...."

Yes, exactly that, but the switch to me feels like a three-way phenomenon.

How do you mean?

In that between a physical world and a dream world is a further augmented world, exponentially swelling in granular influence and intelligence. The physical world became dormant, and thus, reduced stimulation propelled the dream world to prominence, mirrored by hyperevolution, or, should I say, interevolution of the virtual world, where physical matter began to hinder us, and look now, here we are, walking together, unseen. Dream world became real world.

And virtual world became a dream world with all its aliveness and layers of orchestration?

That is what I think.

I see.

You don't sound convinced.

I am thinking, I take my time.

You do.

It is a little like this garden—to fall into allegory (or not even).

What is, Manto?

The virtual world you talk about.

How so?

Not everyone can enjoy this garden, smell its range in early summer. Smells that pop like colours. You and I can walk these grounds because we cannot be seen.

This is true. These grounds are private. Yet, the flora can never be tamed.

Others may not pause at this bench and sit with the warmth of this deep-green bush with purple blossoms. I do not know what it is called.

How did we come to control nature that it could be distributed only to a few?

You and I can walk and be amongst this, what we call 'nature'. We can enjoy it, revel in it, but our experience would be somewhat different if we could be seen.

As we would not be expected to pursue such…leisure?

Yes. We would make for a strange sighting out here, you and I, just walking, placing our feet amongst rocks and reeds, maybe collecting edible berries from down below.

If we could be seen, they would ask, or at least ask themselves, why we are here. After their cultivation and delineation of what wants to grow and contribute freely to our survival, we would disrupt their understanding of how the unkempt world is supposed to look.

Except what we decide to call nature does not care about this, and desire for complete control of the uncontrollable is closer; the mathematical fabric of nature is prone to mimesis. Though I think we know who lies closest to the red earth.

This is due to a code built around a type of body and using time as a weapon, suggesting this body is alien to this natural environment.

And yet it is, in fact, the opposite.

Indeed, here lies the power and violence that can exist in words.

The chicken struts around the yard, its feet kick through red earth, it pecks at morsels, seeds cast down by trees above. It knows the most fruitful corners. Hands pick up fallen papaya, just landed. It is warm to touch, only slightly bruised, perfectly ripe. When cut, the colour of its flesh is as vivid as the red earth; its warm juice dribbles between the fingers of these hands. Two young boys clasp half each of the mango as they stroll slowly away from school down the dusty road. A farmer yells. The boys glance across the street and laugh at the man drying in the sun, reminding them, or one boy in particular, of the dried fish to later be stirred into the stew by the caregiver of the other boy, who will be happy of his laughing friend's presence for a time, but then he must leave, go home before the sun is low. He will hear his mother's angry call bounce across the mesh of small streets housing everyone, from tithe collectors to the unfortunate.

So, the dream about your father?

Oh yes. The fight or the image of the fight intrigued me. I woke thinking about that duel, who won and what role art can play in self-nurture in the absence of a parent at the crucial stage in one's emotional and cognitive development. What that space of inquisition, experimentation, and expression does to offset or even exacerbate the care and the paternal moulding one would typically receive during the years when one's body and mind are tender, vulnerable, forming, and sensitive to all around?

A bit like the dog and its overloaded senses.

A bit like, yes, but that heightened sensitivity is the default for the dog, and rather than living just fifteen or so years, we, or at least I, thickened up, developed a kind of emotionally suppressant exoskeleton against the world to survive. The art for someone without a parent offers a space of solace but not comfort, which feels out of reach.

It doesn't seem comfortable to be compelled to forever search, to ask questions forever.

It isn't, yet this is where I am and this is why the clarity of this symbolic juxtaposition of artist and father in my dream affected me. The artist, or art, against the father. Symbolism almost too obvious, but it never left my mind.

We can shape diptychs from almost anything.

Isn't it dangerous to just see what we want to see? The easiest thing to see is that which is opposite.

You are quiet, Manto.

I quietly agree with you.

I see. There is the possibility that some years ago, the artist and my father had been acquainted. They might have moved in similar circles. As if a trace was left on the ground where they had walked and convened. A trace for me to sense and maybe follow. When I met the artist, an older man, but not quite as old as my father, he looked directly at me and asked me who my father was. It was only later I wondered why. It may have been something he saw in my face. An echo.

Like your art knew your father, even if you did not?

Or my father knew my art. Geological accumulations. Legacies taking root, shaping one's body.

You make me think of an artwork I created many years ago for a small exhibition.

I didn't know you were an artist, Manto.

'Artist' is not a word I would use to describe myself. This was a long time ago. I was quite young.

Though I should have guessed.

I had always hoped, naively, art could exist without the unwieldy sack of patronage weighing upon its shoulders.

Like Christian from *The Pilgrim's Progress*.

Yes, quite like. Besides, I hate that word.

Which word is that?

'Artist'. It is hard to see the essence removed from its yoke; capital. Then when unable to separate from capital, it leads to the trail of subsumption, which begins all the way back at the planet's resources. How does one's soul express itself without becoming the crop of harvest?

I do not have an answer for this.

Neither do I. Many jostle for position to be the chosen crops, harvested and processed, their essences absorbed and set aside to accrue wealth built out of a seemingly infinite resource; us and our need to be heard, to respond to the world around us—a world that has monetised this very anguish—to ask those questions. It is hard to be an 'artist'. You lose a lot. Such as your ability to discern the exploitation in which you need to partake to find raw materials for tools you will need to hack at the red earth to shape your work—which will be purchased, finely packaged, dust removed, in pristine form, though lying within that piece you have produced, will be a familiar feeling, like something manifested in an ancient voice that has always spoken through layers of soil and unforgiving clay. Still, you never listened, you only utilised the ground, shaken loose by the timbre, the vibrations, from this voice you do not know, and you stepped daintily to your delectable lords and ladies and presented your offerings, virtually, nothing to sully the hand, nor to mark the soul.

Your words got me thinking about accumulations within the body and memory or how much we are unwittingly exposed to that we absorb. The artwork I created was of words only. I filled a room with words, papering the walls and ceilings with fragments of conversations I had found, recorded, and written down from my walks around the city. To me, the city had another topography that created meaning simply through language that seemed lost, but to me, it wasn't. These words hung and floated through the air like tufts of pollen in late spring, resting on blackened facades of buildings and on our faces or on the cropped lawns of the city's parks. The words rose up with the smoke from barbecued jerk chicken and weed and white sneakers sullied by the day's end, embraced by a dub sound system and a bobbing knitted hat coloured in stripes of red, gold, and green. They drifted over groups huddled closely together outside bars in the cold, sharing cigarettes. So much has gone.

Interesting.

Should we walk this way, towards that tree?

Which tree?

The one over there, which looks dead but probably isn't.

Yes, OK. These words. I see what you mean. They are everywhere. Silence is rare, if not impossible.

Sentences seemed to lie in everything, and this is, vainly, what I tried to locate within the work I was producing. What would the billboard say to you or me, and how would that message differ depending on the recipient? Based on their respective histories, what would be the recipient's understanding of that combination of words? I thought about what words lay in the flesh of a recently deceased pigeon. The pigeon's body was spread out on the hot black tarmac, recently demolished by a vehicle, I assumed. Its body was opened as if prepared, in the way we might spatchcock poultry for a barbecue, for the opportunistic magpie that takes advantage of a moment's quiet between currents of traffic to pick at the fresh flesh of the pigeon. What words lay in how the magpie cockily stalked the pigeon's flayed torso, strutting around its body in ritualistic dance before pecking at the most exposed, tender spot? It did so in disregard of passing pedestrians who watched through their disgust.

What was it the passing pedestrians said?

What did they say, and where did those words go? How were those words retained in their bodies, and where did they reappear? I found many moments like this and jotted them down without context. No descriptions, dates, or addendums. Just the words, just the incomplete sentences. I liked to look at language for what it actually is, or was, before it is over contextualised to the extent we expect of how to read and receive it. What immediacy it can have when delivered straight from the body.

I like the sound of this.

I would expect you to, of all people.

So words papered the walls and the ceiling?

Yes. There was one visitor to the exhibition I will never forget. She spent possibly two hours there, reading every word.

Every word?

Every word. I watched her from an adjacent room. She entered the exhibition space cautiously, as people do. In this case, it was understandable. En masse, the room looked like well-type-set insanity. I would estimate her age at around forty, though the way she moved implied someone older. It was the middle of a weekday, so there were few visitors. She placed her bag gently against the wall at the entrance, then walked into the centre of the room and seemed to take a deep breath as she looked around at the covered four walls and ceiling. She stood like that for a few minutes, contemplating, it seemed. After a time, she walked back to the entrance, peered closely at the lines of text set in a relatively small size, and slowly inched her way systemically around the space. There was a lot to read. She crept around the four walls and then squinted at the type on the ceiling, which was set larger to make it legible for anyone that chose to look up.

She seemed to trace each line with her eyes and sometimes even with a finger. She'd raise an index finger, and it would hover a couple of centimetres away from the papered wall. I realised after a while that she had committed to the entire experience. At no point did she hurry. Occasionally she would pause and return to her bag. There was a flask in her bag. She would pour out a little tea, just a couple of sips' worth. Before she drank, she would hold the cup for a moment and look around. Then she would drink the small amount of tea, return the flask to her bag, and continue where she left off. During this time, no one else had entered the gallery, so the way she engaged with these words, with this work, went uninterrupted. I sat in the next room, a projection room that worked as a kind of mezzanine, as the gallery was part of an old independent cinema. I was able to look down and see her through a small window. She never noticed me, or at least she never let on that she noticed me. I wondered whether she was really this interested in the fragments of conversations, or whether this was some kind of performance. I could not know. I watched as she claimed these reclaimed words and how they accumulated within her in a way that could only differ from my experience of the same words. I had probably spent more time with them, taken agency in deciding how and in what order I wanted these fragments to appear, but never altering the fragments themselves. They were written down exactly how I heard them; many were likely misheard. When I encountered these words, they were immediate. There, I learned something about how and why we pursue ways to speak, and even sometimes, speak to each other.

Why did you stop, Manto?

Stop what?

Stop making.

I didn't stop. It continued in me within things I did and how I related to the world beyond commerce of exploratory thinking.

I think I understand. Did you make anything else?

After that, I walked and saw, and I read.

You didn't desire to create more?

That is a long story.

We have time.

When I was alive, as a young child, I had all those same dreams. What I wanted to do when I was older. These desires weren't so different from those of many others, to be a painter, some kind of artist, to create and build or write beautiful things. This is all I wanted.

Like many children.

Like many.

The child often wants to be—a life full of what fulfils them, the vibrant, exciting world. How else could one contribute to that, but make; to paint, or to write?

Precisely.

I see. As did I for a significant amount of time.

We still do. Tell me more about your father, or if you would rather not, just the fight.

Some clues can lie within a photograph. I could sit with a particular old picture of my parents for hours. They looked happy, then. Smiles were broad for the photograph, arms wrapped tightly around each other's waist. They were dressed immaculately, but in a way that appeared without much effort. My father's brown leather blazer, aged to perfection. He wore a skinny tie and chunky sideburns. He smiled broadly, my mother too, with so much light in her eyes. A new land, a new stage of their lives and after an education that encouraged them to contemplate joy at the possibility of what their life together might become.

Some things corrode the mind but go unsaid. From inside, a chemical process eats parts of us we need to be seen by and support others, namely, our loved ones. And it can be sudden, and the one we considered beloved can the following day be distant and away travelling elsewhere with the current of their mind, leaving the bosom of home and its deep warm fragrances of saffron and ginger. The laughs quickly become few in a way the beloved cannot understand. A flipped switch, a darkened room, alone on a bed, a face wet with tears. Only silence, after a door slammed and the realisation of the beloved, that she is no longer, and like this there is absence, but the mind is in charge of whether love can be expressed. If one cannot read their beloved's actions, how can love be expressed? I tell you I love you, then my body goes cold and does not feel nor respond to what you need. That divergence is difficult to bridge.

How different minds operate?

Yes. The way doom can swallow you whole. The kind of doom lying within, dormant, and can spring forth unannounced like a volcano, but of rage at, well, who knows, twisting directions of one's orbits. We will not know the origin of this doom or how far back it reaches.

Like separating their two children, for example. A father with some untethered devotion to his firstborn, an heir to something left untold, had attempted to flee with, to flee the unsaid and unsayable corroding love, meant to head with his son to the airport, the flights arranged, his new job and new country set out and prepared in the rich desert which sat atop vast oceans of oil. This attempt to flee, to abandon the mother, the wife and the other child were intercepted, and the mother and children stayed together, but the question would be: Was a rupture left there regardless, a dried, hardened scar on their hearts? As in the younger child, the one to be left behind, though too young to understand anything, could that child nonetheless absorb the rejection, metastasising as their body and mind grew, creating little knots of decay within?

I imagine a kind of awakening to uncertainty.

Where the ground shifts beneath one's feet.

Where one discovers that things said into the world can be untrue.

In the absence of the certainty of an object, of a body, we slide into increasing reliance on symbolism, the posthuman age, in the absence of discernible life, at least how we knew it and in the increasing presence of death.

Discernible life?

Yes, how we walked and talked and felt the touch of a feather against our skin.

Ah, I see. Memories. When we walked and wet autumn leaves squelched under our feet, their colour running as if overwatered gouache.

As if they had not begun as independent leaves before they fell.

Are they dead before or after they fall?

They yellow and curl whilst still attached to the branches of the tree.

This does not mean they are dead.

No, it does not.

When they reach the ground they are together, they share colour and whatever remains as their respective bodies decompose, disintegrating anything at any moment, singular.

As we, in fact, amass the dead and the living in data.

But if we do not learn from the dead, who do we learn from?

Learning from the dead is thinking with them. I am not sure we do this well. We absorb them, consume them, forget them.

In that absorption is a kind of remembrance, for better or for worse. The body certainly remembers.

Does yours?

Why do you look at me this way?

Does your body remember who didn't make it here?

You know it does. How can you even ask me that?

Because you never share what is going on inside. You speak with so much fluency about the outside, but I can rarely get near what is within. There is still so much of who you are I cannot know.

Sometimes I wake at night to a silence that I expect to be a cry.

I don't know what to say, I did not mean to push.

How do you speak to the one you never met but have always known? After a time, a hollow time, when everything took on the pallor of a translucent grey, when the smiles from other people's eyes sank in my cold chasm of loss, when my surroundings grew arid, and I could feel no moisture in the air, and strangers became foes. I felt the eyes of children on me as I passed, as if they knew in which direction I looked, as they were not long removed from that world and its acute senses, granular understanding, and excitement. I talked earlier about that world in which the child discovers things before the child even arrives here, and these were things I hoped would be shared with me, and now I guess

I can speak to the child only from afar.

But within.

We speak every day.

And then you left.

I needed to be alone. I hope you can understand that.

I've been thinking a lot about what it means to begin a life that does not then become a life, even if the conception does not happen inside your body, even if the cells divorce from you but find some place in the person you love for this unique journey to begin, the journey into this world.

And what did you conclude?

Thus yet nothing. I am still in the powerful grip of awe— how my instinct, as an animal, as one hewn from this humus beneath our feet, became so primal. How, once I knew, my sense of the world shifted, even there, just in that tiny moment of understanding. Just knowing, just then, something was about to be different, the sense of my being in the world, the way I hovered through it passing lightly, never fully involved in any of its actions. This changed, a change felt throughout my body. Then unwanted warmth like a bruised skull. A deep ache in my stomach, though it wasn't me, but my lover, that carried a life we did not officially know was there and we would never meet. I knew only the phantom of one's life instinct alters, like a reset, like a piece of advice which could feel beyond one's own mind—cosmic even. Wind took tears through the corners of my eyes as I darted through gloam of late summer, two wheels and my legs launching me home to our child, but our child arrived much too early, whether I was late or not. However, my feet met complete rotations on a crank across the surface heading north where my babies sat. One with hair hung low and wet around their face. Tears obscured and flowing, joining tributaries of sweat, and our other baby was not ready. Not familiar. Not cogent of the goodbyes they were to say to the previous world.

Nondescript in a pool of toilet water. Of a form, we could not… our unrecognisable child. Nothing yet to call physical beyond its tiny…nothing, and yet something magnetic was pulling us all up together as a force. We got the order wrong, and there was death before life.

I'm sorry, Manto. I'm sorry my body could no longer speak to you. I'm sorry we both then lived this death alone. Now that our bodies are no more, now that we have given to the red earth, I feel a touch lighter, as if emancipated, as if I began to know the peace of the other world our unborn child tried to tell us about.

We got there, in the end.

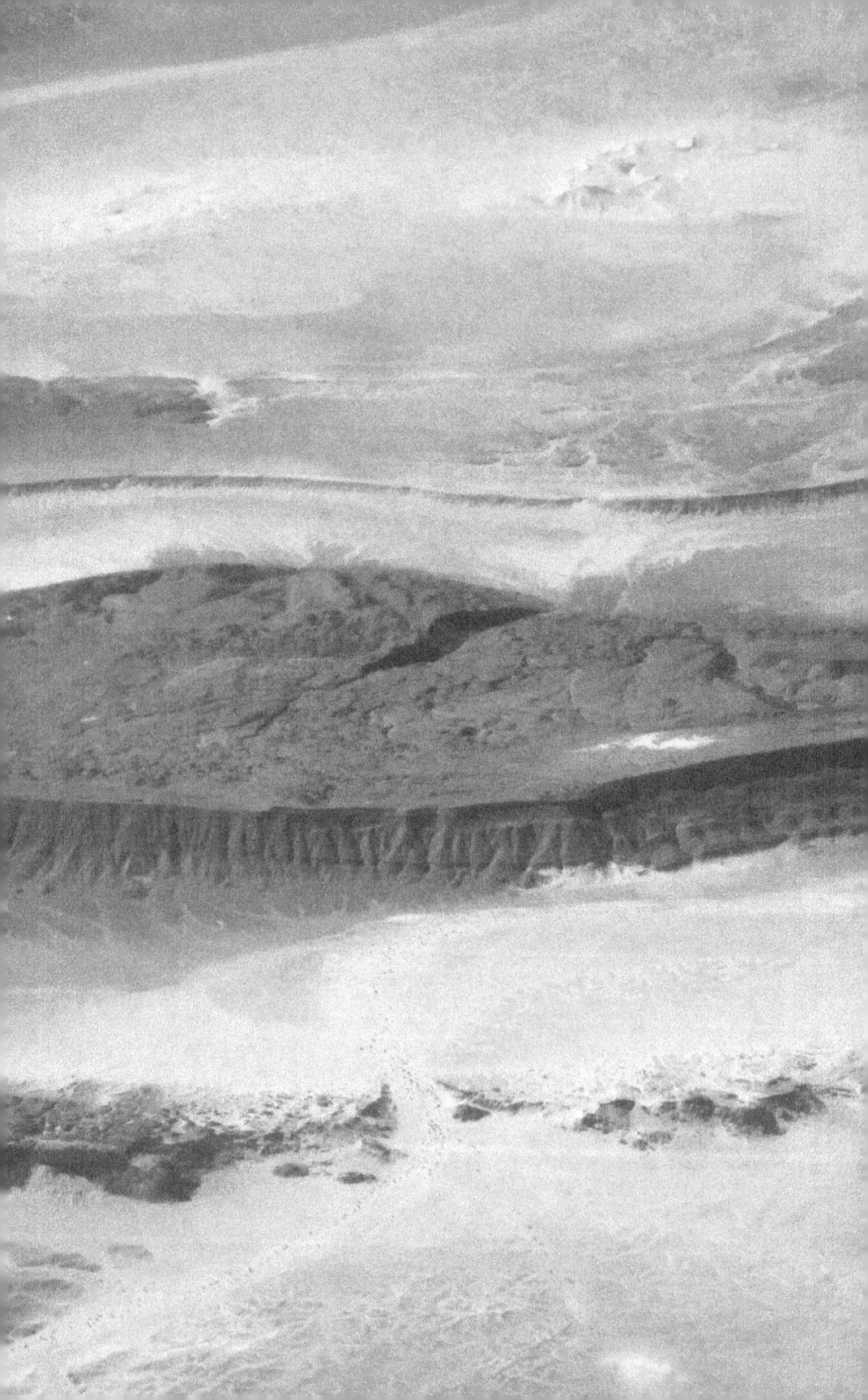

What Lies Beyond the Red Earth?

I will not say too much about the words you have just read, which I hope have left a mark on you. Instead, I'll use these remaining pages to tell you where these words live within the world of *Red Earth*, my interdisciplinary artistic study, combining prose, photography, video, and digital processes. This text is the central pane of (roughly) a triptych of artistic forms, disregarding their taxonomies for consumption. Opening with photography and prose, I discard definitive beginnings or ends and explore several overlapping ideas as I ask whether there's a future for non-Western knowledge systems in a world increasingly structured and determined by probabilistic computation, where statistical models coalesce to decide a chosen narrative for the world. *Red Earth* is ongoing, exploring a diasporic vestibule between cosmologies of thought, cultures and languages and how this 'non-space', which I consider being of nonlinear time, is perceived through an increasingly statistical societal gaze, and how this other world might meet or not with the probabilistic computation crucial to our pursuit of artificial intelligence. *Red Earth* is a question: how can alternative cosmologies be represented within virtual architectures powered by AI innovation?

Transhumanist ideologies of shaky subjective and metaphysical foundations from a singular ontological history imply a determined 'posthuman' future—a future for a human beyond the body's fallibility, a future for a prototypical human based on particular, let's say, characteristics. Colonial legacy is bound within the etymology of programming languages and statistical methodologies widespread in today's revolution of autonomous deities, often of metaphysical and even monotheistic origins. An imposed universal morality derives from this same history of ideas, with little room for other cosmologies of thought in our virtual posthumanity, which is of a centralised moral standard built from selective and, consequently, subjective data. Meanwhile, extraction of natural resources from the African continent and beyond, from rare metals to human data and cheap labour, remains integral to powering the future of increasingly energy-intensive computer hardware and battery-powered technologies aiming to be less reliant on fossil fuels.

A few years ago, I read a lecture by Chinua Achebe given in 1975, later published as an essay entitled *An Image of Africa: Racism in Conrad's 'Heart of Darkness'*. While I greatly respect Achebe's novels, his essays have often left me dissatisfied. His voice reminded me of my grandfather's, the intonations of a proud Nigerian man, rightly aggrieved at the state of his country, his continent, and its indefatigable life in the face of rampant, extractive exploitation and dysfunction from imperial powers. I feel that Achebe's frustration can leave blind spots in his arguments, and the lecture in question, an outright denouncement of Conrad's famed novel and its canonised status as 'permanent literature', was, I thought, an example of this. Achebe considered Conrad's novel explicitly racist in its themes, in its depictions of the 'natives', and in the gaze of Marlow, Conrad's primary protagonist, who Achebe believed wasn't much removed from Conrad's disposition.

Achebe questions the meaning of writing to our society, or the meaning of any art for that matter, which can be so explicitly racist and go mostly unremarked by fans and critics alike, regardless of how beautiful the turn of phrase or evocative the depictions of the lush, sweltering alien landscape. I have a complex relationship with Conrad's novel and agree with some of what Achebe put forth, but his argument felt incomplete. Achebe's disgust is understandable, but I think one can see Conrad was also getting at a lack of vocabulary for this rich, intricate world, of atmospheres and new sensory and metaphysical experiences, at times in his prose defaulting to beautifully phrased but reductive tropes, which are still embedded in the unconscious of Western society today. As Achebe railed at Conrad's reduction of complex cultures, knowledge systems, and languages, down to a dark, flat backdrop for Marlow's descent into the pit of despair, and lamented Conrad's objectification of West African bodies, I became hooked on an important and maybe even existentially rhetorical question—who was Achebe's lamentation aimed at? Who was the primary audience for his words, written in English? And was there a moral authority to hear his appeal, and if so, what then?

I envision this moral authority: a shining round table, a collective ethereal body. I can picture where this body receives education and what information and legacy bestows upon this body to uphold such cosmic authority. I peer at this body's ancestral responsibility and how intricately woven its cultural history is with morality, technology, and progress—through religion, reason, language, war, and subsequent laws, and wonder, wouldn't this same moral authority Achebe speaks to be the same which has canonised Conrad's novel, lauding it as one Western literature's great works?

Roughly around the time of Conrad's birth, Anglican and Baptist missionaries from Britain began spreading the Christian word across Nigeria alongside armed colonial powers, and systemically implemented a proposed order and moral structure, offering bondage under the benevolent cloak of Christianity. They found innovative ways to suppress and diminish ancient local knowledge systems whilst leveraging the local's deeply inherent spiritual devotion. Tribal factions with differing religious and philosophical dispositions were difficult to control without the concerted imposition of particular moral principles through Christianity. Coordinating labour and governing over resource-rich lands was made easier by exploiting the tenets of local knowledge and sowing discord between tribes. Christianity has been significant to psychological governance, by imposing a moral condition and constraining culture, dissenting thought, or ways of seeing and being alien to the new 'explorers' of this productive continent of vast cultural and environmental diversity.

Christianity existed in Africa before the arrival of missionaries. However, their spectral presence served a particular economic purpose, the legacy of which I witness today on the continent and across its diaspora. We can see this coercion and its resulting conservative legacy of docile communities as part of a colonial extraction strategy.

Many early contributions to foundational mathematics originated in Asia and Africa, and roughly a century before these missionary expeditions, the origins of European statistical mathematics and probabilistic methodologies were forming. These methods are now pivotal to computational methods like machine-learning, vital to the pursuit of AI. Bayes Theorem, for example, a formula founded by the reverend and early statistician Thomas Bayes, is a significant driver of machine-learning and originates in what appears to be shaky, metaphysical, and even monotheistic beginnings, as Justin Joque explains in his book *Revolutionary Mathematics: Artificial Intelligence, Statistics and the Logic of Capitalism*.

Bayes Theorem is a mathematical formula for determining conditional probability: the likelihood of an outcome occurring based on a previous outcome having occurred in similar circumstances. One might establish a belief, and later update said belief with newly acquired information supporting one's argument or intention. Bayesian influence is significant to quantum mechanics (which is key to AI research and development) and its attempts to understand the physics of nature and the uncertainty of the universe.

As Joque says, the metaphysical origins of Western statistics have been well-documented by mathematicians and historians alike, many of whom have strongly resisted the Bayesian method, particularly in the twentieth century. Still, intriguingly, this method has recently resurged and is now very popular in algorithmic computing, developing 'truths' (the outcome of this subjective method), principally for capital from numerous subjective origins (including social origins), which, over time, we have established for primarily economic purposes. This subjective Bayesian method, beginning with a guess or an assumption, and adding data to solidify one's guess or assumption, inevitably puts us in a slippery metaphysical dimension, not too dissimilar to where we might have been in years gone by, particularly in Europe, where society leaned on monotheistic reasoning to make sense of the world. Therefore, one might speculate that the logical endpoint of computation based on this statistical model, implemented by engineers and venture capitalists educated under a singular ontological framework, might aim at a convergent 'truth', whatever that may be, if we understand the (even unconscious) influence of monotheism on these protagonists implementing their dominant beliefs and morality, through the accumulation of vast amounts of information, with origins already hazy.

So then, a moral authority? As we use—and I consider this pronoun necessary here, for several reasons, as our involvement purports to be passive, but is not—algorithmic models to determine who has access to a loan or whether someone is guilty of a crime or not (to be then placed in for-profit prison systems) does morality, or a moral authority, as we understand it, ultimately serve only the acquisition, maintenance and accumulation of capital? If so, then to who is the moral vanguard Achebe appeals to?

Achebe's appeal, deep into the latter half of the twentieth century, is to an English-speaking, educated authority, of a dominant economic and educational system, with culture prominently in its service. Hundreds of years of Christian influence and legacy intersect with the Enlightenment's emphasis on reason and individualism, which allies with violent methods of implementing extraction in distant lands in ways increasingly invisible to us as technology surges, all which combine to form today's Western world, where race, class, and gender make for active feedback loops to further accumulate capital by manipulating datasets, which entrench and dictate our respective fates within this socially-constructed economic system.

The same system of imbalances and inbuilt gaslighting narratives provide much of the patronage of art and culture. Patronage that attempts to uphold a moral centre, guiding us to how we might exist alongside each other. 'Culture' defines society's artistic and intellectual refinements. We needn't disregard the etymological origins of the word in this instance; of cultivating and tilling earth until it is fruitful and beneficial enough to sustain life; or the biological, an environment suitable for the growth of bacteria to spread indiscriminately. Culture maintains primacy for this economic system, affirming a dominant language and knowledge and suppressing other influences and dissent. Culture's power and intentions are even crystalline in how few works of literature from across the world are translated into English until they're deemed worthy of translation by an authority, the same, ultimately, which canonises Conrad's *Heart of Darkness*. I remain, for example, astounded by how many contemporary novels from the United States I read with a complete lack of a 'non-white' person written into their pages as if they simply didn't exist. An observation I make with some understanding of the history of segregation, yet, even so, when I imagine the scale of such autonomous formulations within society, it is enough to take one's breath.

Transhumanism, a new ideological formation which appears to be just a loose cluster of ideas, aims at an optimised human condition, which transhumanists might argue can only occur in a state beyond the fallibility of the corpus, where we find empowerment in new deified technologies, which construct a mirror of increasing sophistication. As Narcissus gazes down at his rippling reflection, it begs the question of who stands visible in the mirror. Transhumanism, the technological ascension of the human condition, an idealogical aspiration, appears incapable of imagining ascendency without the ballast of wealth enabling further advancement, inevitably in the hands of a few then tasked with designing the human through a lens which cannot be anything but eugenic by its very foundations. Peer from their vantage point to a tier just below, where our modern saints, namely celebrities, serve as prototypes through feedback loops of continuous visibility and modification, guiding the surface-level aesthetic ideal of the human.

The fervour for AI's ascension to a plane beyond us is a quasi-spiritual desire, echoing the past's metaphysical anxieties and our need to see something, possibly something monotheistic, beyond ourselves. It seems now, through probabilistic methods, the hallowed saint forms in our image as we shape greater systems of knowledge to further a delusion, synthesising the spectacle of an impressionistic all-seeing and all-doing deity and, yes, a moral authority to whom we'll perform worship through mimetic ritual. This supposed moral authority remains a primary weapon for today's technological and economic shackling and extraction from the human condition. Social-media companies, for example, from the same moral lineage discussed here, provide us with ways to see more of the world than ever before but attempt to control what aspects of humanity we should see and aspire to and how. Utilising long-established economic imbalances, these companies maintain what we might call cognitive call centres, across Africa and Asia, paying employees a pittance to screen harmful content before it reaches us, the comparably wealthy consumers, and making it clear, if ever we choose to avert our gaze from the gleaming totem, whose welfare is regarded as valuable and profitable. It has been widely reported that social media has worsened our collective mental and emotional welfare as a society, so consumers also find themselves to be an extractive resource. Then there is our evolving echo, Language Learning Models, and the moral limitations they apply to what we may ask of them. We remain docile to technology, and lack the vocabulary to really speak about it, as Heidegger once noted, therefore we do not or cannot resist.

So I wonder what these universal claims to a moral authority are. How do we determine objective truths about humanity that we lean on to maintain and evolve society, gleaning and reconstituting subjectivity, increasingly informing and guiding our day-to-day, when these truths are developed, in part, through aggregating and reconstituting data, deploying subjective methodologies, which neglect the thought, methods, and experiences of large swathes of the human and nonhuman world, whilst simultaneously finding those realms materially valuable.

I am not saying anything new, but the conditions of diaspora, existing in the vestibule as it were, offer unique perspective and experience, enabling one to see what remains outside 'progress', leaving one room to ruminate on what idealised progress can only mean. Look at the uncanny horror of a slick image export from a Language Learning Model, and see our collective pursuit of an ideal self-representation. This representation of the human, with lines and scars smoothened, feelings transcended, through our loop of dreams and desires, told and untold, live and evolve in billions of datasets, some of which (like porn) tell more truth about what we covet (or think we covet).

The vast processing power and conducting qualities of rare metals required for increasingly energy-intensive computers, from GPUs for gaming and 3D rendering, to the violently wasteful, yet invisible, energy-sapping crypto-mining, ignorantly shilled by celebrities, become a painful metaphor for our wasteful annihilation of the planet. These resources include human data and labour, and despite many obstacles, the African continent gains increasing attention from swarming venture capitalists for its young, growing middle-class, tech-literate population and technological innovations.

Diverse languages, as with diverse tribes, existed beyond and across the dividing lines of nationhood engraved throughout the continent by colonialism, but language control has since been one of the most effective ways to control land for access to resources. One can hear lamentations at the reluctance of African teachers to teach in native languages and who even reprimand students for speaking them. When we comprehend what else language suppresses, such as cultures, knowledge systems, and distinct moral principles, which may differ from the standard fed to us, we might think differently about the accelerated consolidation of languages, meanings, and intentions, output by our digital deities, a homogenisation echoed by reduced agricultural biodiversity.

As Ngũgĩ wa Thiong'o says, to be divorced from one's mother tongue is a form of slavery, and language is more than a simple ordering and patterning of words or signs, but it runs deeper, through the body, through the soil and a continuous lineage of ancestry in dialogue with the earth. Many former colonised countries grapple with the in-between—the metaphysical struggle between imposed and inherent cultures and the disingenuous contradictions of a top-down moral design. How do we consider how 'native' English speakers of formerly colonised countries use the language differently from what we might consider the standard?

So we reach the bubbling core of *Red Earth*, which is no lament—quite the contrary, it is a meditation from a particular vantage point, even if I am partly divorced from my mother tongue. I am a fluent 'Listener', but I cannot confidently be a 'Caller'—which, for me, is a strange vestibuled condition, an incomplete relationship to a native cosmology, swirling only at its fringes, one's body feeling and intuiting, but rarely articulating this innate knowledge, even though I hear it, and feel it, like the red earth between my toes, and in how the sounds of palm leaves rustling say so much more. I ask what this kind of in-between means for a world of precise statistical perspectives and binary ordering. I can see and feel what posthumanity has existed in this culture and what lies beyond the soul-sapping postcolonial discourses, where many wail and others nod along as if listening, but not really. What lies beyond? With my feet firmly planted on the ground, I try to touch this possibility, however faintly.

I grab this vestibule, an open secret, as a unique place of my own. Born to Nigerian parents and raised in the United Kingdom, I submit to the perpetual translation of my identity—a constant feedback loop, charging back and forth from one cosmos to the other. Growing up, this became a distinct private space removed from many other people in my immediate environment. Rather like the way I have existed between cultures, languages, and knowledge systems, I have wondered if there is any possibility of creating a dialogue between probabilistic computation based on the origins mentioned earlier and the metaphysical foundations of alternative origins, such as, in this case, Yoruba culture. Or is the idea entirely paradoxical and pointless? The diasporic existence, a meshing of worlds across time and space, traversing coordinates, existing in motion, non-place, and uncertainty (a realm also concerning quantum mechanics), is an interesting point at which to consider where and how knowledge systems and language might meet, or to consider at least any impressionistic or metaphysical entanglement with these knowledge systems—mathematics in dialogue with ritual and tradition.

Famed Nobel laureate playwright and novelist Wole Soyinka addresses such parallels in his book *Myth, Literature and the African World*, when he posits the many similarities one could draw between Yoruba deities and the 'universal relevance' of Greek gods significant to the origins of Western thought. One of the temporal concepts Soyinka addresses is the nonlinear conception of time beyond the human, a key concept in Yoruba thought and philosophy and a key driver to *Red Earth* and the prose you might have read. Soyinka suggests Yoruba is comparable with Greek mythology, or Judaeo-Christian theology, in richness and depth, and how, for Yoruba, the degree of acceptance of something like nonchronological time is implicit, innate and given reverence and understanding. Within such thought, one can also find moral dispositions, actions, and practice differing from those in the Judaeo-Christian or Greek mythological definition of the term, where, for instance, the Greek gods, as Soyinka explains, are beholden to little or no consequence for their depravity. The only time they may bear consequence is when they infringe upon another deity, unlike the Yoruba deities, who commit transgressions, but must somehow acknowledge their actions. Soyinka suggests the existence of an alternative morality to the European, which may, to a large extent, be unconscious in Yoruba society. Yet, when I consider my diasporic vestibule, I consider these unconscious realms and how these subtleties, which are part of me, and others in our behaviour and language, disappear in universalising computational concepts.

With *Red Earth*, I have created a speculative meditation on what equitable exchange between culture and computation could become, where I include different modes of translation, in a continuous, nonlinear process to draw attention to the need for new archives of the future and new ways to think about a computational existence. Early experiments with GAN (generative adversarial network) machine-learning translation models (language-to-image), which were born of the probabilistic methods mentioned earlier, made me wonder whether a kind of virtual visualisation of distillations from a space between cultures and ideas was possible. Or is computation, by its foundational principles, anathema to other metaphysical dimensions than the one from whence it came? As words drive my creative practice, I decided to eke out a metaphysical realm of my own, from which I could begin a process of experimentation, an interdisciplinary practice echoing my reality.

As you might have guessed, the name *Red Earth* comes from the prominence of red clay earth forming much of West African land towards the equator. This colour results from the earth in this region being enriched by iron and aluminium, oxidised by the elements, and this earth cannot typically grow crops as it is. It must undergo a series of processes to do so, an alchemical practice of organic transformation, which goes back a long way. This process becomes a metaphor for my artistic translations between forms, an illustration of crossing knowledge systems, languages, and literary sources. I am less concerned with specific objects of beauty or a particular output or goal; my focus is on continuing thought, idea, and language through forms—evocative of Yoruba nonlinear experiences of time, through the body and beyond—the body's relationship with time and space, nonhuman environment, earth, fauna, and flora. I aim at a process in dialogue with the machine, but a process I can control, rather than simply allowing automated input and output. I collaborate with and disrupt subjective machine processes, rather than passively receive automated direction. Hence my instinct to first write a work of prose in its entirety, which I can use as the earth of these experiments.

I begin with photography, which I use as note-taking to think through a moment or assist in sketching an idea. Though vernacular in a sense, the photographs hold some artistic resonance as I apply a subjective interpretation to both taking and reading them. In this case, I translate what I read in them (without a machine), and they become the first in a series of interlinked forms. As I took photographs at different coordinates across three continents, I began to see time and space in the narrative, a prose piece which might travel through the material and virtual dimensions. I considered the juxtaposition of dynamic mathematical infrastructures within physical matter (from living flesh to the formation of geology over time) and how we travel over these structures when moving or migrating, with the immediacy of emotion and instincts, like fear and doubt.

You will no doubt catch the strong influence of Dante in this work, and, not least, epic poetry. I aim at a humble dialogue with this tradition, to think through my meandering ideas and existence, responding to *The Divine Comedy's* vivid metaphors, journey, and engravings of a world. After I wrote this prose, I flowed it through the rest of the project, in physical and virtual spaces, in exhibition spaces and digital artworks, translating small fragments and embedding them in sculptural forms, which eventually became objects computationally imbued with my information, and more. This engagement with the Yoruba experience of time seemed parallel, in some ways, with virtual time and space—the virtual existing everywhere and nowhere, the immateriality and abstraction of a coordinate.

I used the prose to experiment with code in the form of early language-to-image translation models, where the outputs from the prose were rudimentary swashes of colour and shape. The models tried but failed to read into my subjective musings, which were insufficient for literal outputs. The prose disrupted with its metaphysics and uses of metaphor. At the time, this inability of the models to accurately synthesise my subjective inputs was the most interesting part of this process, certainly when considering the 'truth' at the heart of these models. What and whose truth does the computer aim for?

Having worked in 3D for several years, I've long been interested in the potential of time-and-space simulations and how this extra dimension echoes how non-Freudian cultures engage with dreams. So I took the translation process further, combining another model to create an input mesh from the image data to create 3D meshes with vertex displacements (vertical variables in a 3D material which create form and texture), which have formed based on coordinates found in the generated image data, from changes in colour and shape, where the model has attempted to calculate some compositional representation of my prose, almost like weather forces, allowing them to form circumstantially as a kind of alternative geology in which the materials or skins are full of the prose data. With 3D software, I manually combine these skins and their built-in topographies, virtually sculpting a series of symbolic structures evocative of Yoruba totems, computationally imbued with meaning, messages, and sometimes specific stories, where virtual forms have amassed my prose and linguistic data, embodying the text, offering a hyper-codex—embodied language and metaphysical ideas filling each object or symbol.

Red Earth is self-referential, even in how I am reflecting on the access I have to tools and software powered by the same extraction. I think about how these sculptures I have created might live within compositions, even within virtual architectures, either narratively artistic or simply as archives of language and heritage. This evokes how Yoruba culture manifests meaning and stories in material objects through ritual and gestural demonstration. I place these sculptures within my photographs, a kind of violence in the purgatorial space between ideas of self and origin that I have and that others might have on my behalf—language as an abstract imposition, continuing the agitated, disruptive conversation I am having with the past and the future of colonial hierarchies.

I've little interest in creating artworks where a seductive aura is embedded within the definitions and form of an object. I am much more interested in indulging in an open theoretical space, where all these forms become relational nodes forming a collective thought. In some works, I am actively working against the vernacular of material and seduction, instead working with the ephemeral instantaneity of digital processes and their strange data permanence, like what is left to us by the dead, responding to the same boomerangs of data in our technocratic processes, which seem to seal our respective fates. Video is one of the forms I use for this study and I approach it like painting, moving back and forth between worlds, the virtual incarnation of the discord coming from restricted access to culture and language. I try to hint at infinite open worlds, at least for a moment.

Red Earth is a speculative exercise about language and data, and whose language, history, authority, and morality are now encoded into our digital realities. I am asking if our current trajectory will only entrench the negation covered here in feedback loops much faster and more granular than we can comprehend, and whether there is any room at all for provenance with this data or is it inherently flawed. Is this simply the underwhelming and even violent trajectory for the autonomy of alternate cultures, moral ideas, and outlooks as their lands of origin shudder and succumb to climate damage? Are these works rhetorical aberrations or possibilities?

References for *What Lies Beyond the Red Earth?*

Achebe, C. (2010) *An Image of Africa.* Penguin Classics, 1st ed, London.

Joque, J. (2022) *Revolutionary Mathematics, Artificial Intelligence, Statistics and the Logic of Capitalism.* Verso Books, London/NYC.

Soyinka, W. (2008) *Myth, Literature and the African World.* Cambridge University Press reprint edition.

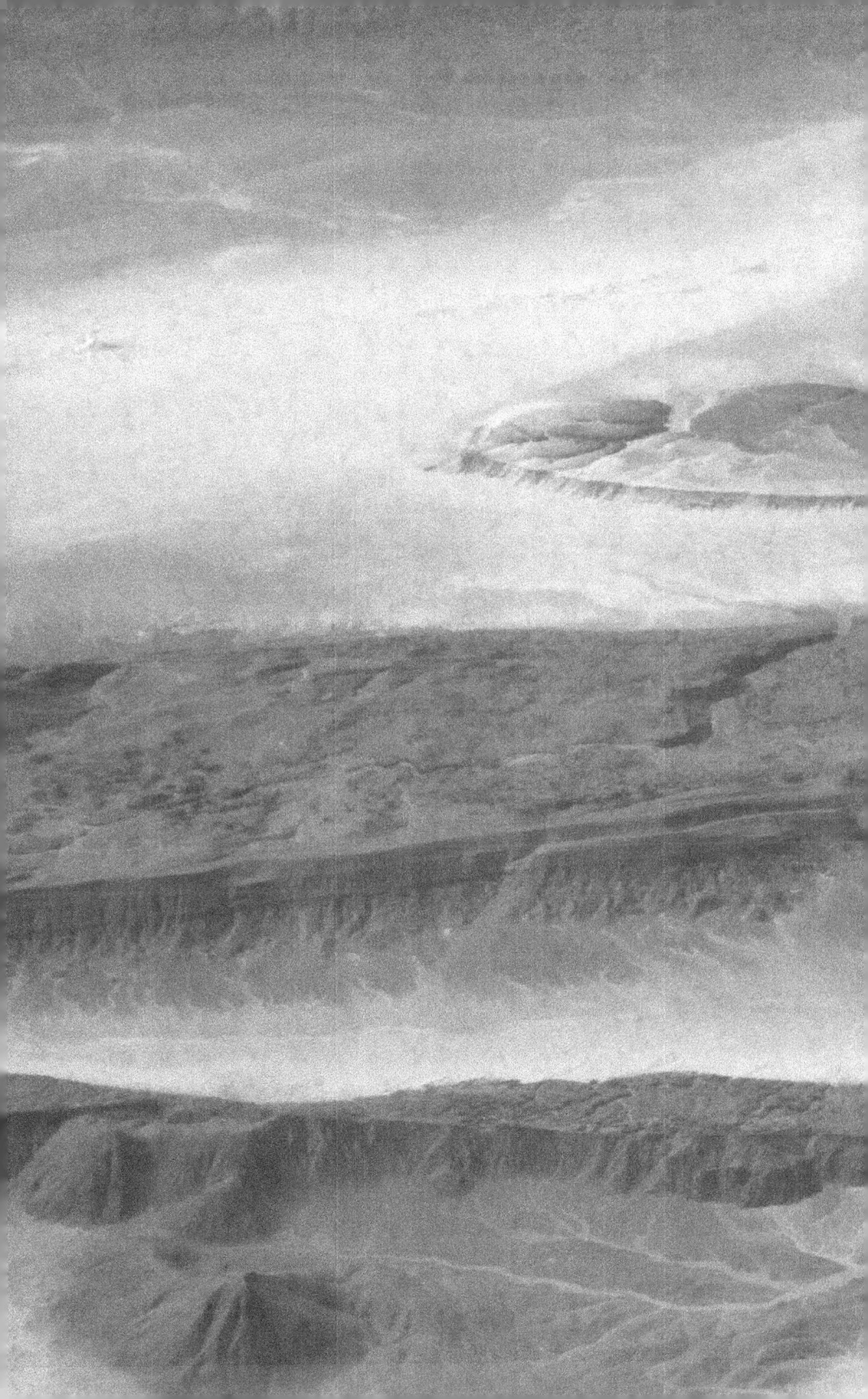

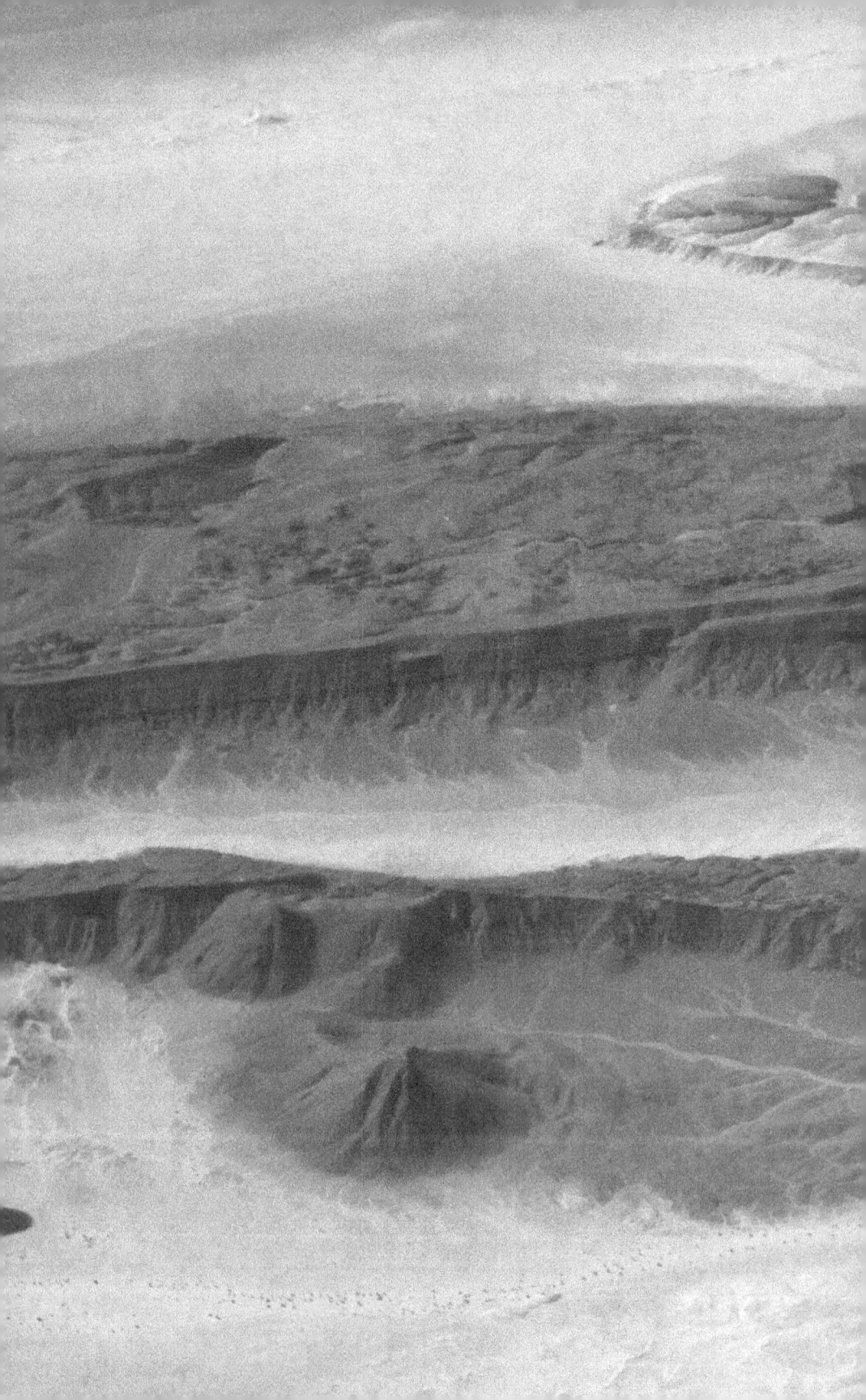

www.ingramcontent.com/pod-product-compliance
Lightning Source LLC
Chambersburg PA
CBHW051316220526
45468CB00004B/1362